THE CYCLIST'S FRIEND

THE CYCLIST'S FRIEND

Copyright © Summersdale Publishers Ltd, 2011

With research by Chris Turton and Jennifer Barclay

Illustrations by Kath Walker

Summersdale Publishers Ltd
46 West Street
Chichester
West Sussex
PO19 1RP
UK

www.summersdale.com

Printed and bound in the UK by CPI Mackays, Chatham ME5 8TD

ISBN: 978-1-84953-146-7

Substantial discounts on bulk quantities of Summersdale books are available to corporations, professional associations and other organisations. For details contact Summersdale Publishers by telephone: +44 (0) 1243 771107, fax: +44 (0) 1243 786300 or email: nicky@summersdale.com.

THE CYCLIST'S FRIEND

A MISCELLANY OF WIT AND WISDOM

ILLUSTRATIONS BY KATH WALKER

CHRIS NAYLOR

CONTENTS

INTRODUCTION

I can think of no sincere, decent human being,
male or female, young or old, saintly or sinful,
who can resist the bicycle.

WILLIAM SAROYAN

For many people cycling is synonymous with happy early memories of a first bike; the special sense of achievement felt when finally managing to make it to the end of the road without veering off into a hedge is one of the defining moments of childhood. For those who choose to continue their love affair with the bicycle, this feeling never fades: the thrill of locomotion, the joy of working in tandem with an ingenious machine and the knowledge that a new world is only a few pedal strokes away.

There are approximately twice as many bicycles as cars in use across the world today – and with escalating road congestion, sky-high fuel prices and the threat of global warming, travelling by bike is an increasingly sensible option. The National Cycle Network is now responsible for 12,600 miles of cycle lanes, main road routes and traffic-free cycling paths in the UK, meaning that there's never been a better time to get on your bike.

OK, so you may have to occasionally wrestle with an oily chain, negotiate unruly roads and bear the brunt of some truly awful weather, but what you gain from cycling is, as John F. Kennedy once put it, a 'simple pleasure'; an uncomplicated machine, with a basic principle, to be enjoyed in the simplest of ways.

This miscellany, for anyone who enjoys cycling at any level, is filled with quotes and excerpts from across the centuries, with carefully selected trivia and practical information, collected here in celebration of the genius of the bicycle.

To me it doesn't matter whether it's raining or the sun is shining or whatever: as long as I'm riding a bike I know I'm the luckiest guy in the world.

MARK CAVENDISH

EARLY REVOLUTIONS

When the spirits are low, when the day appears dark, when work becomes monotonous, when hope hardly seems worth having, just mount a bicycle and go out for a spin down the road, without thought on anything but the ride you are taking.

Arthur Conan Doyle in *Scientific American*, 1896

HIGHLIGHTS IN THE HISTORY OF BICYCLE INVENTION

1817: Baron Karl Drais von Sauerbronn, who trained in technology at the University of Heidelberg, Germany, invented the wooden 'running machine' or *Laufmaschine*, which was patented the following year in France.

1839–40, Scotland: a blacksmith, Kirkpatrick Macmillan, designed and built a machine in which power was supplied to the back wheel via rods connected to treadle-type pedals.

1843, France: Alexandre Lefebvre created a rear-drive machine, said to be more sophisticated than Macmillan's; he took it to America and it still exists in the History San José museum.

1866, USA: Pierre Lallement, a Frenchman working in the USA, got backing from an investor, James Carroll, for his 'Boneshaker' and was granted the first patent for a pedal-powered two-wheeler.

1870, England: Inventor James Starley produced the 'Ariel' High Wheeler (aka 'Ordinary' or 'Penny Farthing') with hard, solid rubber tyres. Later versions had front wheel sizes of up to 5 feet. The large front wheel reduced the chance of lodging in potholes.

1885, England: John Kemp Starley (James Starley's nephew) and cycling enthusiast William Sutton marketed the revolutionary Rover Safety Bicycle with a chain/rear-sprocket drive and tangentially-spoked wheels. It had many of the major features of modern bicycles but with solid rubber tyres. The Rover is recognised as the first commercially successful bicycle and is credited with being the major force behind the 'bike boom' of the 1890s.

Think of a new idea in bicycle design and someone will have already invented it, probably in the nineteenth century.

JOHN PINKERTON, ENGLISH CYCLING HISTORIAN

When man invented the bicycle he reached the peak of his attainments.

ELIZABETH WEST, *HOVEL IN THE HILLS*

MOUNTING A PENNY-FARTHING

To many people the penny-farthing may seem to be a ridiculously impractical contraption, not least because its high front wheel makes it appear to be extremely awkward to mount. However, if you take a closer look you will see that most high-wheelers feature a foot peg a few inches above the smaller rear wheel. With handlebars gripped and one foot planted on the peg, riders could push off for some initial momentum, then pull themselves up onto the saddle and pedal away. Of course, penny-farthings didn't have brakes, so dismounting was a little less graceful!

TYRED OUT

Before rubber, the first versions of tyres were bands of metal or wood. The word could be derived from 'tie', referring to the outer ring that ties the wooden spokes together, or from 'attire': its origins are obscure.

In 1844, Charles Goodyear discovered the vulcanisation process that enabled rubber to retain its shape in hot weather and yet remain flexible in cold weather; perfect for bicycles. Within a few years, bicycle tyres were made of solid rubber. Meanwhile, engineer Robert William Thompson of England acquired a patent for the concept of the air-filled tyre, but his was made of a canvas inner tube and leather outer, called the Aerial Wheel, and was not developed commercially.

The first practical pneumatic tyre was made by Dr John Boyd Dunlop, a vet from Scotland, while working in Belfast in 1887. The story goes that he created it for his son's bicycle to prevent the headaches he experienced riding on rough roads on a 'Boneshaker'. Dunlop created the first commercial pneumatic bicycle tyre in 1888. A year later, Frenchman Adolphe Clément-Bayard saw the tyre in London and acquired the French manufacturing rights for 50,000 francs. In 1891, the Michelin brothers patented a removable pneumatic tyre.

Cycling is now society folks'
favorite pastime.

NEW YORK TIMES, MARCH 1885

LIGHT MY FIRE

In the early 1930s, British cyclists used 'carbide' lamps. Lumps of calcium carbide were placed in the bottom chamber. Water was then dripped onto it from the top chamber, and a gas was given off which was lit. Made of thick glass and fairly heavy, the lamp fastened onto the bike on a hinged bracket. A trick to stop them going out when you hit a pothole was to wrap a bit of wire around with the end in the flame; this would glow red and would re-light the gas if the flame went out. In this period, cyclists didn't use rear lights, but only reflectors.

TOOLING UP

*Marriage is a wonderful invention: then again,
so is a bicycle repair kit.*

BILLY CONNOLLY

While many riders revel in the thought of a new all-singing, all-dancing cycle computer, complete with satellite navigation system, heart monitor and perhaps even a novelty *Knight Rider* interactive voice panel, such accessories could be seen as an effort to take cycling into unnecessarily 'techy' territory. On the other hand, any innovation or accessory that makes life easier without damaging your patience or your bank balance is surely welcome, and many of them are indispensable to basic bike maintenance and enjoying your riding in comfort.

THE BARE ESSENTIALS: MAINTENANCE

Cleaning Kit: Whatever type of riding you do your bike will pick up grit and grime. Giving your bike a regular and thorough clean will not only keep it looking good, but will also allow its working parts to keep on working as they should for longer. Specially formulated bike-cleaning fluids are a great idea, especially for those who like to get down and dirty off-road. Using a cloth rather than a brush on your frame will reduce the risk of scratches, though your chain and other lubricated parts will need a good scrub with a brush. Regularly degreasing and re-lubricating the chain in particular is sensible, as this will reduce wear to the chain ring and cassette or sprocket and prevent rust. Rims and brake pads are two further areas that are vital to keep clean.

Lubrication: Ensuring your bike is properly lubricated is also necessary to protect its working parts from excessive wear and tear. Teflon-based spray lubricants are ideal for keeping the smaller parts of your bike working smoothly, and have the added bonus of creating a light, water-repellent seal when used on areas such as your (rim) brake mechanism. Traditional 'wet' oil is considered best when it comes to greasing your chain. There are companies – such as Green Oil (www.green-oil.net) – who produce non-petrochemical lubricants, meaning you can be environmentally friendly while looking after your bike.

Essential Tools: Despite their differences in design, most contemporary bicycles are held together using bolts and screws that require an Allen key. As such, a selection of Allen keys – widely available in the form of an all-in-one tool – is vital for everything from removing a wheel to adjusting your brakes, headset and saddle. Tyre levers are pretty much essential when it comes to removing your tyres efficiently.

Maintenance Accessories: A track pump – which can take the huffing and puffing out of inflating your tyres at home – is a great idea, whatever style of riding you're into. Many come with pressure gauges, meaning you can correctly inflate your tyres for optimum performance.

The cyclist's best friend – the puncture repair kit – is something you should never be without (unless you're riding on 'self-healing' tyres filled with goo!).

After a good deal of study of catalogues I decided on a Raleigh Pioneer Elite but by the time I had made up my mind it had gone out of date and become last year's model. This did nothing but good. The young man who runs the local cycle shop explained that bicycles are a matter of fashion like motorcars [...] Everyone wants the latest model or the latest bicycle, and as the bicycle makers cannot always think up technical advances every year they generally just change the colour or the trimmings and call it a new improved version.

EDWARD ENFIELD, *FREEWHEELING THROUGH IRELAND*

WHAT IS IT WITH CYCLISTS AND LYCRA?

Many a wisecrack or muted snigger can be heard from the uneducated friend or bystander when they are faced with the sight of your inny and outy bits on show in your brand new Lycra cycling gear. To those not in the know, such a deviant fashion statement is all but incomprehensible – unless (guys) you happen to be Linford Christie. However, the fact is that cycling and Lycra go together like Sundays and roast dinners, and for good reason. First off, cycling shorts are close fitting, which reduces your wind resistance and makes the job of getting around less of a struggle. The tightness of the shorts also has a compressing effect on the leg muscles – which helps prevent fatigue. The material is stretchy and non-abrasive, meaning the risk of chafing is considerably reduced. Furthermore, Lycra is good at wicking away sweat from the skin, the effect of which helps to cool the rider down.

So when you look at it, you can't get much more sensible than spandex. Well, sort of...

Cleaning a bike's like cleaning a toilet. If you do it regularly, it's fine and easy. If you wait, it's a truly disgusting experience.

STEVE 'GRAVY' GRAVENITES

BITS AND PIECES...

- Beginning as an auto parts outfit in 1923, American company Bell Sports are responsible for what was arguably the first purpose-built cycle safety helmet, the 'Bell Biker', released in 1975.

- Currently, the use of a safety helmet while cycling is not mandatory for riders of any age in the UK. Despite the seemingly obvious benefits of having a protective layer around the head, there is substantial evidence from the UK Department of Transport against the idea that cycle helmets reduce the risk of head injury.

- In an attempt to gauge how motorists reacted to cyclists of a different sex, traffic psychologist Ian Walker of the University of Bath conducted an experiment which involved him cycling in a wig to give the impression to approaching cars that he was in fact a female rider. His study found that the wig kept cars at a greater distance than when he cycled without it!

THE BARE ESSENTIALS: IN THE SADDLE

Helmet: Although there is evidence both for and against the argument that cycling helmets definitely make riding safer, the reassurance of having something to protect your head if the worst should happen and you have an accident means it's surely worth strapping one on – even if it does make you look like a B-movie spaceman.

Saddle Bag: Whether on your back or on your saddle, you'll need a place to keep – at the very least – your puncture repair kit and your pump or other inflation device. In addition, a spare inner tube is a wise way of coping with a complete blow-out. Carrying some funds for emergencies is also a good idea. If you have a mobile phone it is worth taking it out with you, though it will probably be better off in your jersey pocket, since your saddlebag will be subject to a considerable amount of road vibration while attached to your frame.

Portable Inflation Device: For fixing punctures on the go you'll need some way of inflating your tyres. Portable pumps range from the annoyingly unmanageable to the impossibly small, but for a truly pocket-sized solution CO_2 inflators are the way to go.

Gloves: Something that improves your grip on the handle bars can never be a bad thing. For long-distance road riders padded gloves are a godsend; even if you're not into functionality, a pair of cool-looking gloves can simply be a stylish addition to your cycling wardrobe. For riding in low temperatures – when the wind chill factor makes you feel as if your fingertips have been flame-grilled – you will be deeply grateful for some insulated gloves.

Suitable Clothing and Footwear: This very much depends on your style of riding, but there are a few general rules to abide by if cycling regularly:

- Laces are bound to get caught up in your pedal mechanism, so Velcro is a good option.

- Loose-fitting and flapping clothing is likely to make your ride harder.

- Clothing that features reflective or hi-viz elements is a must when riding in low-light conditions.

- You bear the full brunt of the weather when it turns bad while cycling, so be prepared by kitting yourself out with some wind and/or waterproof gear.

There's no such thing as the wrong weather, just the wrong clothes.

SCANDINAVIAN PROVERB

CYCLING AROUND
THE WORLD

*When I got back from my bicycle trip across
France people asked me, 'Which was the best part?'
'The cycling,' I replied.*

EDWARD ENFIELD, *FREEWHEELING THROUGH IRELAND*

After a century and a half, the bicycle has reached all but the very remotest of locations. European cities such as Amsterdam are teeming with cyclists, with around 30 per cent of its citizens' trips being made by bike. Travel to Tianjin in China and you will see around 77 per cent of people using pedal power – easy to believe when you consider that in 2000 alone China produced 52 million bicycles. At home in the UK, citizens are more modest with their cycling, with the figure for bicycle use standing at around 8 per cent.*

Despite what the figures tell us, it is clear that the bicycle is still a firm favourite both for leisure activities and daily chores, and for those fortunate enough to be able to experience how bicycles are used abroad, one can be sure that, whether in Texas or Timbuktu, you'll never be too far away from one kind of cyclist or another.

* SOURCE: JOHN PUCHER, *TRANSPORTATION QUARTERLY*

THE WORLD'S MOST CYCLE-FRIENDLY CITIES

Davis, California: whose city logo is a bike, must rank somewhere near the top. With a population of only 65,000, it boasts over 100 miles of cycle lanes and paths as well as bike tunnels, so 17 per cent of residents commute to work by bicycle. Residents of Davis voted to phase out public school buses years ago, encouraging children to walk or cycle to school, and the university is virtually car-free. A bike map is displayed throughout the city. Visit in May for the Cyclebration, which goes on all month.

The flat terrain and moderate temperatures in Davis help its citizens embrace the bicycle, certainly, but other cities have also found clever ways to make themselves more cycle-friendly, such as designated lanes and signals and sufficient safe parking. Here are some other places of note for cyclists:

Portland, Oregon (USA): the 'Create a Commuter' scheme provides low-income adults with commuter bicycles (including lights, lock, helmet, pump and more).

Trondheim, Norway: the world's first bicycle lift, inspired by ski lift technology, carries cyclists uphill.

San Francisco, California: all public transportation has been equipped to carry bicycles.

Berlin, Germany: riders have access to 390 miles of bike paths, and online route-planner 'BBBike' (www.bbbike.de) determines the best bike route between two points in Berlin. You can even choose to avoid cobbled streets, unlit paths or traffic lights!

Barcelona, Spain: a 'green ring' surrounds the metropolitan area with a bike path. Green is also the colour used to name the Vias Verdes ('green ways'), a network of disused railway tracks that have been converted into cycling and walking tracks that run for 1,500 km throughout Spain. Over 58 tracks allow riders to take in some spectacular scenery, including age-old viaducts, rocky mountains and even tunnels once used by the trains.

Vias Verdes

In the distance, the patchy green mountainsides were peppered with bright yellow broom, while beside the road and the dirt tracks that joined it, swathes of white alyssum, smaller patches of blue rosemary and even isolated, hesitant, pink rock roses were bringing life back to the land.

RICHARD GUISE, *TWO WHEELS OVER CATALONIA*

Most bicyclists in New York City obey instinct far more than they obey the traffic laws... Cycling in the city, and particularly in midtown, is anarchy without malice.

AUTHOR UNKNOWN, FROM *NEW YORKER*, 'TALK OF THE TOWN'

THE WIDE, THE TALL AND THE BEAUTIFUL: SOME EXOTIC BIKE RIDES AROUND THE WORLD

Langkawi, Malaysia: think water buffalo grazing, back roads leading to secluded waterfalls, white sandy beaches and verdant jungle... Langkawi makes for pretty laid-back riding.

Port Phillip Bay, Melbourne, Australia: the bay is like a great seawater lake, with a coastline 160 miles long. Basalt plains give way to granite hills, tortuous ascents and stunning views.

Jotunheimen National Park, Norway: this is the highest mountain area in Scandinavia. The crystal views of still mountain lakes along the way make strenuous climbs worthwhile. Or try the Sognefjord Cycle Route between Borlaug and Turtagrø: it combines mountains and fjords with fewer hills.

Uyuni salt flats, Bolivia: if you love wide open spaces, try Uyuni for swathes of white salt, baked hard under a blue sky. Night temperatures sink to around −20°C (−4°F). Make sure you have fat tyres.

Gorges de la Jonte, Cevennes, France: in autumn, as you cycle with vultures circling above, the trees clinging to the steep sides of the Jonte gorge put on a riotous display of colour.

Whitehaven to Sunderland, UK: traverse England from sea to sea at its thinnest point through the Lakes, the Pennines and the Dales, around 140 miles from start to finish.

CYCLING AT THE OLYMPICS

The international spirit of cycling is perhaps represented nowhere better than at the Summer Olympics, where cycling events have created some of the sport's most memorable superstars. From home-grown talent, with the likes of Chris Hoy and Victoria Pendelton, to other modern-day greats from across the world, such as Switzerland's Fabian Cancellara and Australia's Cadel Evans, competitive cycling at this event enjoys a high profile.

Today's Olympics fans may, however, be surprised to know that cycling featured in the very first modern-day Olympics in 1896 in Athens. Six events (Road Race, Sprint, Time Trial, 10-km Race, 100-km Race and a 12-Hour Race) were based at the Neo Phaliron Velodrome, three of which – the sprint, time trial and 10 km race – were won by French cyclist Paul Masson. This was to be the start of France's international reputation as a producer of world-class cyclists.

Variable gears are only for people over forty-five. Isn't it better to triumph by the strength of your muscles rather than by the artifice of a derailleur? We are getting soft. Give me a fixed gear.

HENRI DESGRANGE, SPORTS JOURNALIST AND
WORLD TRACK CYCLING CHAMPION

FAMOUS RIDER: VICTORIA PENDLETON (1980–)

Victoria Pendleton was born in Bedfordshire in 1980, and has steadily risen to fame as Britain's most successful female track cyclist. Her father, Max, was a British national grass-track cycling champion, who achieved cycling's ultimate honour – featuring on the cover of *Cycling Weekly* – multiple times. It was he who inspired and encouraged Victoria into the sport, seeing talent in her at a young age. Taking her to watch cycling races every Sunday, and modifying his tandem so that she could ride on the back when she was just six years old, she cites him as one of the reasons for her success: 'Dad pushed me; wanted me to fulfil my potential, and I wouldn't have got to where I've got to without him.'

She quickly began to garner achievements on both national and international stages, winning several world championships and setting four world records. Her coach once claimed that she was 'too skinny, too puny' to be a sprint cyclist, but her feminine image and long hair are something she is intensely proud of – and they haven't stopped her going on to become one of the world's leading female track cyclists. She is credited with bringing a touch of glamour to a previously male-dominated sport and making it accessible to the general public for the first time thanks to her likeability and popularity in the media.

The secret to her motivation is a system of personal rewards; she says, 'If I hit 200 rpm on the track behind a motorbike, I'm, like, "yes!", and will probably reward myself with extra cake for tea.' Eating whatever you fancy is one of the perks of having such a demanding training routine, but for Pendleton, a pure love of cycling is what keeps her going: 'When the sun's shining in the morning and you get up it's a joy to go out on your bike.'

ROCKY MOUNTAIN WAY

*Great things are done when men
and mountains meet.*

WILLIAM BLAKE

BITS AND PIECES...

- The name 'mountain bicycle' first appeared in print in 1966.

- A mountain bike (MTB), otherwise known as an all-terrain bicycle (ATB), is designed for any off-road cycling, from dirt trails to tree-strewn mountain passes.

- The sport became popular in the 1970s in Marin County, California, USA – a history covered in the 2007 documentary *Klunkerz: A Film About Mountain Bikes*.

- In the late 1970s and early 1980s, companies started to manufacture mountain bikes using high-tech lightweight materials, such as M4 aluminium.

- The first mass production MTB was the Specialized Stumpjumper in 1981.

- The Mountain Bike World Championships – cross-country and downhill, for men and women – started in 1990.

- Short cross or speed cross (SC), a new form of mountain biking, is riding narrow forest paths with rocks and roots to distances of up to only a few hundred of metres – a sport with extreme speed, skill and thrill.

PASS-STORMING

In the 1930s and 1940s, a craze known as pass-storming took hold. A book of the time – Harold Briercliffe's *Cycle Touring Guides* – devoted to cycling in the Lake District described certain mountain passes as 'rideable' or 'negotiable' or 'emphatically not rideable', but said that tackling Scarf Gap and even the Sty and Esk Hause, 'is a thing apart and known as pass-storming'. The idea was to ride your bicycle as far as you could up mountain tracks and carry it when you had to, to reach the steepest and harshest terrain, before careering down again. A thing apart, indeed!

Wrynose Pass
Cumbria

The secret to mountain biking is pretty simple.
The slower you go the more likely
it is you'll crash.

JULIE FURTADO

When you ride hard on a mountain bike,
sometimes you fall; otherwise
you're not riding hard.

GEORGE W. BUSH

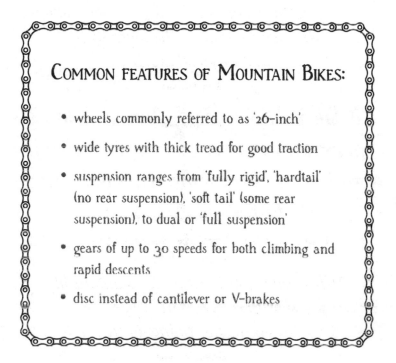

COMMON FEATURES OF MOUNTAIN BIKES:

- wheels commonly referred to as '26-inch'

- wide tyres with thick tread for good traction

- suspension ranges from 'fully rigid', 'hardtail' (no rear suspension), 'soft tail' (some rear suspension), to dual or 'full suspension'

- gears of up to 30 speeds for both climbing and rapid descents

- disc instead of cantilever or V-brakes

If I'm in Texas and there is a local mountain bike race, will I go down and do it? Probably... I'm committed to the bike for life!

LANCE ARMSTRONG ON CYCLING AFTER HIS RETIREMENT FROM PRO ROAD RACING IN 2005

THE OFF-ROAD FAMILY

Cross country (XC): emphasis on climbing, speed and endurance - bikes that are lightweight and efficient, often with full suspension. Not for steep or severe terrain.

'Trail' bikes: development of XC with less of an emphasis on weight, and built to handle rougher terrain.

Enduro/all-mountain (AM): for all-day rides involving steep climbs and steep descents.

Downhill (DH): the most 'sag' for traction to go fast over bumpy trails.

Freeride (FR): similar, with less emphasis on weight and more on strength, for technical downhill trails.

Trials: no suspension, often no seat, very light; have multiple gears for competition, but many riders use one fairly low-speed, high-torque gear.

Dirt-jumping, urban and street: between a BMX and a freeride bike, very strong, low seatposts and oversized handlebars.

FAMOUS RIDER: GARY FISHER (1950–)

Gary Fisher, at the age of 24, built the first ever off-road bike which was capable of riding up mountains as well as down – his customised Schwinn Excelsior X. It was his pioneering use of several new modifications which created a whole new sport, which he was to christen 'mountain biking' in 1979 when he named his new company 'MountainBikes'. Discussing the new craze, Fisher said, 'It was a big hot secret, like a new drug. You'd turn someone on to it and they were like "Wow I've gotta have some of that. I gotta have one of those." It was intoxicating.' At the time, racing enthusiasts regularly competed in the downhill Repack race on Mount Tamalpais in California; a precipitous road which descended 1,300 feet in two miles, so-called because the hub coaster brakes on the bikes would get so hot that the grease would evaporate and have to be 're-packed' for the next descent. In 1977, Fisher set a record of 4 min. 22 sec. for the course, which still stands today.

Fisher had been competing in road and track races from the age of twelve, although he was forced to take a four-year hiatus from 1968–72 when officials suspended him from competing because his hair was 'too long'. He went on to win a 125-mile Olympic Development race, the Tour of Klamath Lake in 1976, the 209-mile Davis Double Century, and in his later years, the demanding Transalp 8-day off-road race. However, it is his innovative vision in the world of bike design for which he is renowned. His bikes have been included in the 'Top Ten All-Time Best Mountain Bikes' by *Mountain Bike Action* magazine, and in 1987 he was named as one of the '50 Who Left Their Mark' by *Outside* magazine. In 1988 he was inducted into the Mountain Bike Hall of Fame, and in 1994 he received a Lifetime Achievement Award at the Korbel Night of Champions. Such accolades are the result of years of hard work, making countless improvements to the way mountain bikes are manufactured, with his own-brand bikes now being sold in more than twenty countries worldwide. Even today, Fisher still rides, races and looks for new trends and improvements for the mountain bike frame, and has been recognised by *Popular Mechanics* for his innovations in sports.

LEAN, MEAN
RIDING MACHINE

*Honestly, bicycling isn't just fun and healthy
and non-polluting, it's sexy. It gives
you a nice rear end.*

MATTHEW MODINE

CYCLING FIT

- Bicycling uses all the biggest muscles in your body: quads, hamstrings and hip and gluteus muscles.

- Long, steady rides build capillaries in your legs, so you can deliver more oxygen-rich blood to your muscles. The fitter you get, the more oxygen you can use, and the more fat you can burn.

- Cycling burns through the calories. At a pace of 13 to 15 mph, you burn 500 to 600 calories in an hour. After cycling, your body continues burning calories while it works to repair and replenish muscles. It builds lean muscle tissue and raises your metabolic rate, and because it's energising, you're likely to be more active all day.

- Biking decreases the visceral fat around your organs that can lead to heart disease, diabetes and other health problems.

- As little as 10 minutes' cycling can improve your mood, and 30 minutes a day several times a week can even relieve the symptoms of depression, as well as helping you to get a good night's sleep.

- Have an easy 20-minute ride before breakfast to burn an additional 1,000 calories a week and turbocharge your fat-burning metabolism.

IN FOR THE LONG HAUL

You may feel proud when you reach landmark distances when starting out on your bike – 25, 50, 100 miles – and rightly so since these are all worthy achievements, but there are those out there for whom the ultimate goals lie not just over the hill but over the horizon, in a different time zone. To Brits like Rob Penn – who took three years to ride 24,000 miles around the world, Mark Beaumont – who broke the round–the–world record in 2008, and Vin Cox – who completed his world ride in just over 163 days, pedalling from Land's End to John o'Groats might seem like a trip to the corner shop.

Spare a thought, too, for the athletes who compete in the Race Across America (RAAM), an 'ultra marathon' in which teams ride day and night to cover the breadth of the country on their bicycles, from east to west (3000 miles), in around a week. Despite the event's daunting distance, it attracts some interesting and unlikely competitors; in 2009 Rage Against the Machine bassist Tim Commerford formed part of Team Surfing USA, along with surf legend Laird Hamilton.

STRETCH IT OUT

Whether you're planning to go for a 5-mile cruise to the local pub or a 50-mile training ride, warming up with a series of stretches is sensible. Lightly stretching the groups of muscles you'll be using while riding will ensure you start off the ride in a relaxed state, as well as preparing your mind for exercise.

Converting calories into gas, a bicycle gets the equivalent of three thousand miles per gallon.

BILL STRICKLAND

EAT, DRINK AND BE MERRY

It's easy to put off taking cycling to the next level and making it more of a way of keeping fit than a hobby, especially when you encounter super-fit, super-disciplined, 'I do thirty miles to work and back on a daily basis' riders. Luckily, for those of us who like to enjoy life's many little indulgences, there is much evidence to suggest that having a little bit of what you fancy does not always detract from your performance on your bike.

Drink Wine and Feel Fine: A study conducted by the Institute of Genetics and Molecular and Cellular Biology in Illkirch, France found that resveratrol – a nutrient present in red wine – increased the distance test mice were able to run. Although cyclists are more than a tail and a whisker apart from a mouse, the findings suggests that a night at the pub needn't ruin your ride.

Indulge your Sweet Tooth: At Indiana University, USA tests showed that drinking chocolate milk before a ride was more effective than the specially-developed energy drink Gatorade in providing fuel for riding.

In the early days of the Tour de France, before scientifically formulated energy drinks and power bars were invented, an off-the-shelf bottle of Coca-Cola – which contains energy-replenishing sugars and performance-enhancing caffeine – was perhaps the most highly prized pick-me-up a rider could get his hands on. That, and amphetamines, which were widely used by competitors before testing was introduced.

Call in the Love Doctor: It is widely known that sex encourages endorphins, which have been observed to have a pain-killing effect. As such, getting frisky with your partner might be the ideal way to soothe those post-ride aches: just tell them it's doctor's orders!

IDEAL PRE-RIDE SNACKS:

- Banana and yoghurt
- Cereal and milk
- Crackers and peanut butter
- Fig bars and milk
- Oatmeal and raisins

ADAPTED FROM *RIDE YOUR WAY LEAN* BY SELENE YEAGER

As a youth I'd just jump on my bike and be off , but some eight years earlier on a charity bike ride across Cuba, I'd joined in the stretching exercises insisted upon by our leaders every morning, often before a crowd of giggling Cubans peeking around their doorways. With about eighty Europeans of all ages, shapes and sizes togged up in multicoloured Lycra, I think anyone can imagine the gigglesworth of the sight.

RICHARD GUISE, *FROM THE MULL TO THE CAPE*

REMEMBER...

For any bout of exercise proper hydration is also key so remember to take a drink before setting off. Don't overload yourself, though, or else you'll be making an early pit stop!

And remember: eating a balanced diet gives your body the best start when you undertake exercise of any sort. It can be useful to eat cycling-friendly foods to help you get the most out of your ride, but don't forget to maintain some variety in what you eat – otherwise you'll take the enjoyment out of it.

Man's Most Efficient Vehicle?

In *Toward a History of Needs*, Austrian philosopher Ivan Illich pronounces the bicycle 'the perfect transducer to match man's metabolic energy to the impedance of locomotion', seeing modern society's ever-increasing need for speed in transport as misguided.

Illich discusses the efficiency of the bicycle at length, explaining that, when we break down the bicycle's ratio of energy spent to distance travelled, 'man [on a bicycle] outstrips the efficiency of not only all machines but all other animals as well'. This is no doubt an impressive statement scientifically speaking, but not exactly reason enough to trade your shiny, twin-injection Porsche for a pushbike!

For Illich, the value of efficiency is not just down to thermodynamics but, more importantly, politics: using the 'right tool' (one that shows the most all-round efficiency for the task it's designed to do) for the job means that as individuals and as a society we get things done in a more logical and sustainable way. According to this argument, for the task of transporting oneself from A to B with all-round efficiency – from the energy spent in locomotion, to the effort required to produce and maintain the machine, to the adaptability of the vehicle to travel over different terrains and routes, to sheer availability – the bicycle cannot be bettered.

Cyclers see considerably more of this beautiful world than any other class of citizens. A good bicycle, well applied, will cure most ills this flesh is heir to.

DR. K. K. DOTY, IN *HOW TO BICYCLE*, 1892

Punctures, Patches and Perseverance

On a bicycle, you never have the wind with you – either it is against you or you're having a good day.

DANIEL BEHRMAN, *THE MAN WHO LOVED BICYCLES*

So there you are with your finely tuned bike in full working order, gliding happily along a quiet country lane, the sun shining, the birds singing and the delicious thought of a pint and a pub lunch slowly simmering away in your mind, when all of a sudden your daydream and your ride begin to steadily lose momentum and sag, with the dreaded sound of air slowly hissing from somewhere below. And – what luck! – in all the excitement of the prospect of a perfect day's riding you forgot to check if you had your puncture repair kit in your bag, and by some cruel twist of fate the spare inner tube you have with you is the one you meant to throw away after your last repair. The pub is another 5 miles away and chances are they don't have 10 mm-square rubber patches and tubes of vulcanising fluid on draught. Once again (it is undoubtedly not the first time) you've let the temptation of simply 'getting on your bike' get the better of you.

Even in the most idyllic of scenarios, cycling can turn from dream to disaster in an instant – *if* you're not properly prepared. Having the right kit and the know-how to deal with the kinds of challenges you'll face when riding is just as important as having a fully functioning bike.

CHECK ONE, CHECK TWO

There are some basic checks that should be undertaken before every ride, especially if it's going to be a long one. More serious mechanical issues should be checked for and addressed before the day of your ride, but it's worth giving your bike a once-over just before setting out.

Tyres: ensure that your tyres are correctly inflated according to the pressure quoted by the manufacturer (usually printed on the sidewall of the tyre). A quick squeeze can tell you if your tyres need more air, but ideally you should use a pump that has a pressure gauge.

Brakes: give the brake levers a pull to check the mechanism is working smoothly. If they feel soft it will pay to take 5 minutes to adjust them. Be sure to check all bolts are tightened properly if making any adjustments.

Fixings: during the course of riding it's possible for bolts, screws and other fixings to work themselves a little loose. Pull out your Allen key and give them a test, especially if you've been working on your bike recently.

*My bicycle had been showing signs of battle
fatigue. The front wheel, which had had three
punctures, began to go 'Bump bump', and the
gear-change was very stiff, so it made my
thumb hurt. Also, I had left the rear light on
after a misty start to the day and flattened the
batteries... In this state I limped into the centre
of a big unattractive town called Rive-de-Gier,
which deserves to be given a wide berth, and
found that its two bicycle shops were,
it being Monday, shut.*

EDWARD ENFIELD, *DOWNHILL ALL THE WAY*

Never use your face as a brake pad.

JAKE WATSON

Refrain from throwing your bicycle in public.
It shows poor upbringing.

JACQUIE PHELAN

RAIN, RAIN GO AWAY

Of all the adverse weather conditions one can encounter while cycling, rain has to be the most uncomfortable. Not only does it make the unprepared rider shiver and wince uncontrollably, it also reduces visibility and compromises the road surface. Here are a few simple things to consider when riding in inclement weather:

1. **Check the weather forecast:** the best way to avoid the inconvenience of wet weather riding is to check whether it's due to rain that day. If your region is expecting a monsoon, chances are it's better to leave the bike at home!

2. **Put on your waterproofs:** you should be able to find cycling-specific waterproof clothing to cover you from head to toe if need be. If you're commuting or touring it may be easier to wrap up more extensively or carry extra kit, whereas if you're doing something more sporty you'll need to travel light. Try to consider what the bare essentials are for your particular ride.

3. **Be safe:** take it a little easier and brake earlier. If you see a surface that looks like it might be slippery, avoid pedalling while passing over it. A peaked cycling cap under your helmet can help keep driving rain out of your eyes.

4. **Be seen:** Hi-viz clothing and lights will help to alert other road users to your presence.

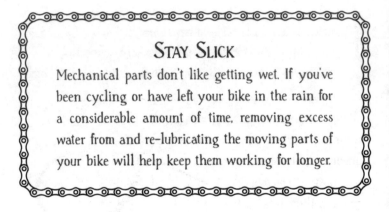

STAY SLICK

Mechanical parts don't like getting wet. If you've been cycling or have left your bike in the rain for a considerable amount of time, removing excess water from and re-lubricating the moving parts of your bike will help keep them working for longer.

ZIP IT!

Plastic zip-ties, available at any good hardware or electrical store, can be used for a variety of emergency repairs – when you find yourself stranded with a broken seat post clamp, for instance. Attaching one or two ties to force the broken clamp together means you can make it home without having to hover uncomfortably above a bare seat post – remember to go easy, though, as a tie is not a substitute for the clamp itself!

THE WHITE STUFF

It may seem a little ridiculous at first, but in fact cycling when snow is on the ground is far from impossible – while trains are at an icy standstill and cars are dancing around like Bambi on ice, you could be steadily and smoothly making your way through the chaos on your bike.

As with heavy rain, there's little point in heading out in a blizzard. However, if you're relying on your bike to get you to work, for instance, it may be necessary to brave the elements, so here are a few tips on making things easier:

- Fit your bike with some off-road tyres (not essential but a big bonus if you can get hold of some).

- Increase your traction by letting a little air out of your tyres.

- Try not to tense up, and keep your weight on your saddle.

- Take it easy, but not too easy as your forward momentum will help you keep your balance on more slippery stretches.

- Brake steadily and take corners gradually.

- Keep a keen eye out for any extra hazards (ice patches, frozen tyre ruts, etc.).

- Don't take unnecessary risks: if the surface looks too hazardous, simply jump off your bike and walk.

I have always struggled to achieve excellence.
One thing that cycling has taught me is that if
you can achieve something without a struggle
it's not going to be satisfying.

GREG LEMOND

There may be a better land where bicycle
saddles are made of rainbow, stuffed with
cloud; in this world the simplest thing is
to get used to something hard.

JEROME K. JEROME, *THREE MEN ON THE BUMMEL*

IDENTIFYING A PUNCTURE

Wherever, whenever and however they happen, punctures are bad news. However, taking the time to examine the damage as you repair one will ensure that you identify the exact cause, and so eliminate any underlying problems that may have been the culprit.

- A bog-standard breach of the inner tube while riding over a sharp object is the cause of most punctures and can easily be patched. It's important when fixing the puncture to remember to check the inner wall of the tyre for any shard or thorn that may still be lodged in there – checking the outer tread for extensive wear and perforations is also a good idea as this is another likely cause of persistent punctures.

- Two small holes close together are most likely the result of a pinch or 'snake bite' puncture, where the inner tube has been trapped between the tyre and the rim when riding over a hard or sharp object – usually due to the fact that the tube has been caught when being fitted or as a result of the tyre not being inflated fully.

- A less common puncture is one to the inner (rim-facing) side of the tube. This will most likely be the result of a protruding spoke head that has broken through the rim tape. A close look at the rim will determine whether or not you need to replace the tape or take measures to correct the spoke heads.

Nobody travels on the road to success without a puncture or two.

NAVJOT SINGH SIDHU

CYCLO-CROSS

If the challenges of cycling in winter conditions appeal, cyclo-cross may be the sport for you. Cyclo-cross is most often characterised as something road racers take part in over the autumn and winter months as a high-intensity alternative to lengthy road rides in uncomfortable conditions. Races are usually between 30 minutes and an hour long and consist of a high number of laps around a 1- to 2-mile course that is largely off-road. Courses may also include man-made obstacles like stairs and low hurdles, which are often tackled by expertly timed dismounts. The bikes used by 'crossers are similar to those used in road racing, but they often have knobbly tyres and cantilever breaks for extra mud clearance. The constant slog of pedalling through damp mud or frozen snow, combined with the incessant wrestling of the rider's bike around ditches, over tree roots and up steep hills, all while trying to keep up an all-out racing speed, makes cyclo-cross a real iron-man sport, understandably referred to by some as an 'hour in hell'.

FREEWHEELING

If I were not a man, I would like to be a bird.
As I am a man, I do the next best thing,
and ride a bicycle.

REV. MALTIE, IN *HOW TO BICYCLE*, 1892

Bicycles have no walls.

PAUL CORNISH

The bicycle is the most civilised conveyance known to man. Other forms of transport grow daily more nightmarish. Only the bicycle remains pure in heart.

IRIS MURDOCH, *THE RED AND THE GREEN*

Although the bicycle has seen many incarnations since it first appeared in its various hulking and impractical wooden varieties in the early 1800s, there is no doubt that at its heart – like all great and revolutionary inventions – it was, and still is, a symbol of the desire to rise above the limitations of everyday life. In the early days, bicycles enabled their riders to overcome the relative hardship of travelling on foot or the cost of travelling by carriage, while later the first women riders made a charge for equality as the first women riders during the Golden Age of the bicycle, and today we're able to simply escaping the confines of our immediate environment on our two-wheeled friend.

This attitude was especially evident in the mid to late nineteenth century, when the phenomenon of the bicycle really came into its own. We need only look at some of the names of the models and makers of the time to grasp just how much bicycles appealed to those with a mind for 'higher things': companies like the Franco-American Bicycle Co. released their 'Falcon', while Peugeot had their 'Lion'; other French companies of the time opted for mythical titles like 'Cycles Gladiator' and 'Cycles Sirius'. Their advertising posters, too, featured celestial beings who appeared to have reached the upper atmosphere on their bikes. Perhaps most significantly, wings – either on the ankles of riders or on the bicycle wheels themselves – featured almost universally in the representation of the bicycle, clearly conveying the idea that with such a machine mind and body could take flight.

For many people today, riding a bicycle is about different kinds of escape: immersing yourself in the exciting and challenging world of bike sports, or just taking a break from the hustle and bustle of town and city life and venturing out into the fresh air and green country landscapes. There are roadies, mountain bikers, tourers, BMXers, time trialists,  commuters, retro riders, leisure cyclists, green activists and everything in between. What they all arguably have in common is an appreciation of the unique feeling of independence that only comes with owning and riding a bicycle.

PEACE OF MIND

Albert Einstein has been widely quoted as saying that his theory of relativity came to him while riding on his bicycle. No doubt a mind like Einstein's was constantly teeming with ideas, but there is also a scientific explanation as to why cycling can be good for your mental health.

Aerobic exercise naturally produces endorphins, chemicals which have pain-killing effects and increase feelings of well-being in the brain and in the body. These effects help to dissipate tension and stress even when you're no longer in the saddle. More involved cycling, like trail riding, will give your mind something to focus on intensely, giving it a break from the worries of everyday life, whereas when you hit the road and just ride and ride your mind often enters a calm but contemplative state, which could give you space to solve a problem you might be dwelling on.

Collectively, the effect of taking regular exercise by cycling means that your mind and body get the respite they need to carry on functioning healthily – and who knows, out on your bike one day it might be you who comes up with the next world-changing idea.

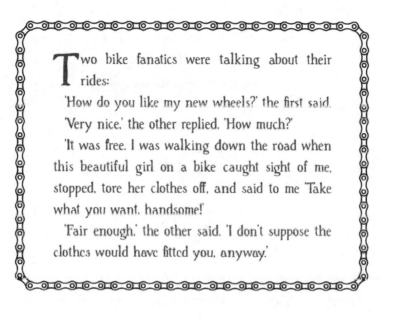

Two bike fanatics were talking about their rides:

'How do you like my new wheels?' the first said.

'Very nice,' the other replied. 'How much?'

'It was free. I was walking down the road when this beautiful girl on a bike caught sight of me, stopped, tore her clothes off, and said to me 'Take what you want, handsome!'

'Fair enough,' the other said. 'I don't suppose the clothes would have fitted you, anyway.'

All creatures who have ever walked have wished they might fly. With highwheelers a flesh and blood man can hitch wings to his feet.

KARL KRON, *TEN THOUSAND MILES ON A BICYCLE*

If the constellations had been named in the twentieth century, I suppose we would see bicycles.

CARL SAGAN

With lifted feet, hands still,
I am poised, and down the hill
Dart, with heedful mind;
The air goes by in a wind.
Swifter and yet more swift,
Till the heart with a mighty lift
Makes the lungs laugh, the throat cry:
'O bird, see; see, bird, I fly.
'Is this, is this your joy?
O bird, then I, though a boy
For a golden moment share
Your feathery life in air!'

HENRY CHARLES BEECHING,
FROM 'GOING DOWN HILL ON A BICYCLE, A BOY'S SONG'

CUSTOMISING YOUR BICYCLE

The bicycle enables us to escape many other machines: we use it for transportation, sport, recreation, and make it a way of life.

JOBST BRANDT

Whether you're upgrading to a slick £3,000 super-bike or simply trading in your clapped-out shopping bike for something that goes more than two miles without voluntarily shedding any of its vital working parts, nothing quite beats the feeling of coming home with a new bike. However, as good as your new machine feels during your first few rides, there will no doubt come a time when you feel the urge to make some adjustments to it – personalise it, adapt it to fit your own purposes, or simply make it more comfortable to ride. The easiest way to do this is of course to enlist the help of your friendly local bike shop, though if you do you may be depriving yourself of some important lessons in getting to know how your bike functions, not to mention missing out on the satisfaction that comes from fixing or adjusting something all by yourself. When it comes down to it, the bicycle is really quite a simple machine and many basic additions and adjustments can be done with the help of a handbook, an online video tutorial and a bit of determination. Of course, customisation isn't just about feeling good; for some bike owners, looking good is what counts, and throughout history cycling has seen some wild and wonderful modifications that have produced some remarkable bikes.

ARE YOU SITTING COMFORTABLY?

One of the easiest and perhaps most beneficial items you can customise is your saddle and/or seat post. For most kinds of riding the saddle is where the majority of your weight rests when riding, so having one you find comfortable is essential. Most likely, you will consider changing your saddle after you've decided it is not sufficiently comfortable. Before deciding to replace it, however, it might be worth experimenting with the positioning as this can make a big difference; also, consider if any other part of your bike could be having a negative effect on your riding position. Once you're sure your current saddle is not doing its job, try to consider what kind of saddle will improve the problem: a wider saddle, perhaps with a pressure-relieving canal, will hopefully provide increased comfort while a narrower saddle will be less obstructing to your pedal stroke. A suspension seat post will help absorb the jolts and vibrations that can be transferred to your bottom while riding, as will a more flexible carbon seat post.

Life is like a ten-speed bicycle. Most of us have gears we never use.

CHARLES M. SCHULZ

RIDIN' LOW

Not many modern bike designs have broken the classic two-triangle-frame mould, but back in the 1963 legendary American bike company Schwinn released their revolutionary Sting-Ray, a kids' bike that had some of the custom-cool stylings of the chopper style motorcycles of the time. With its laidback riding position, 'ape hanger' handle bars, elongated banana seat and extended 'sissy bar' at the back, the Sting-Ray looked almost as impressive as the motor vehicles it was inspired by.

Taking further inspiration from lowriders of the California and Mexican car culture of the time – classic American cars customised with chromed wheels, fenders, etc., which had their suspension lowered so they sat close to the ground – bike owners in the 1970s continued to experiment with modifying their bikes by adding ornate chrome parts and heavily spoked wheels, and stretching them out even lower to the ground.

Today, the lowrider bicycle style is popular throughout the world and offers a chance for owners to express themselves and show their imagination and skill by creating something that is totally unique.

CHOOSING THE RIGHT TYRE

As with most new parts you buy for your bike, your choice will largely depend on what type of riding you do most. When selecting new tyres one essential thing to bear in mind is whether they will fit comfortably on your rim – you will need to consider the rim's diameter of course, but also whether or not the tyres will be too wide or too narrow.

Tread is something that will often come down to personal preference, but it goes without saying that if you ride on the road most of the time, a slick or semi-slick tyre will work best: it will provide less rolling resistance as it will be smoother and have a more uniform surface contact with the road. The opposite applies for off-road riding, which requires knobbly treads to maintain grip over unstable surfaces. Hybrid tread tyres can often cope with different surface conditions, but the best possible scenario would be to have different pairs of tyres to suit different situations.

BURROWS THE BIKE WIZARD

Norwich-based bike designer Mike Burrows is a man synonymous with modern-day bicycle innovations. Perhaps most notably, he's responsible for the revolutionary Lotus 108 time-trial bike, which Chris Boardman used to win an Olympic gold in the 4,000 m pursuit in 1992. Working with Lotus engineering, Burrows advanced the idea of the monocoque (from the Greek *mono*, meaning 'single' and the French *coque* meaning 'shell') bicycle, in which carbon fibre moulding was used to create a light, aerodynamic frame perfect for time-trialling – the first of its kind. The bike, however, was not all that reliable: during the 1994 Tour de France Boardman was reported to have gone through a dozen frames.

Not only was Burrows responsible for a world-class racing bike design, but his innovation and imagination have produced some truly inspired recreational and utility bikes. His design for a folding bicycle – the Giant Halfway – is supremely compact thanks to its monostay (an asymmetrical fork). Another superb commuter bike is his 2D, which is designed to fold flat against a wall, for those restricted on storage space. Other Burrows design marvels include the Ratracer – a super-slick recumbent bike – as well as his 8 Freight – a courier bike with an 8 ft wheel base to spread the weight of the rider's cargo, which can be placed in the spacious area between the seat post and the rear wheel. No doubt about it: Burrows is a genuine bike-design master!

PEDAL ON

Changing your pedals is something you may consider if you find yourself riding longer distances. Clipless pedals offer more efficient power transfer than flat pedals or those with toe clips, since they fix the rider's feet more securely, especially on the up-stroke. Again, your choice of pedal will most likely be determined by the kind of riding you do: mountain-bikers may opt for a hardwearing pedal that is resistant to clogging with dirt, while road riders may go for something more minimalistic and light.

As with the pedals, cycling shoes are designed to suit different needs; one key issue to consider when switching to the clipless system is how much walking you'll be doing in your shoes; shoes designed for mountain biking and cyclo-cross often have enlarged treads for gripping in the mud, while road shoes have smoother soles which are awkward to walk in when you're not on your bike.

Remember that when fitting your new pedals that they will always be marked with 'L' and 'R' to indicate which side they should be fitted on.

THE BLACK LABEL BIKE CLUB

Reputed to be the first ever 'outlaw' bicycle club. Black Label is an international group that combines a love of 'mutant' custom-welded bicycles and cycle-based fringe activities with a do-or-die alternative lifestyle spirit. United by their fierce opposition to the use of petrol-run motor vehicles, the club have been known to take to the streets of New York on their tall bikes – a bike consisting of two frames welded one on top of the other – or wildly extended choppers, and then participate in bouts of bicycle jousting surrounded by riotous spectators, in a sort of pseudo-anarchistic exhibition of their brotherhood. A documentary film. *B.I.K.E.*. was made about the club in 2005.

FAMOUS RIDER: BOB HARO (1958–)

B ob Haro is known as the 'Father of Freestyle'. He was not only the first, and the best, BMX trick-rider of his time, but he also modified and designed the first real freestyle bikes and set up his own company, Haro Bikes. However, none of this might have come about had he not decided to take his motorcycle apart at the age of 16. Haro was already working as an artist for the magazine, *BMX Weekly*, after he was struck by the poor quality of the drawings in it, and sent in some of his own sketches. He was used to motocross racing, but when he ran out of money to put his motorcycle back together, and his dad refused to let him buy a dirt bike, he opted for the next best thing – modifying a road bike to turn it into a custom-made BMX. He began using his riding skills to impress his friends and work colleagues, persistently trying out trick after trick until he had each one honed to perfection. He took an evolutionary leap in the biking world when he invented the world's first flatland BMX trick, dubbed the Rock Walk, in which the rider 'walks' the bike along by pivoting 180° alternately on the front and back wheels, using the brake to keep the wheels still while swinging the bike around for each pivot. Flatland became a freestyle BMX riding craze (described as 'artistic cycling' as it is performed on a flat surface without the use of any ramps, jumps or rails), and Haro soon began touring America and Canada doing shows with his friend Bob Morales.

In 1982 Haro released a bike customised to suit flatland freestyle riding: the Original Haro Freestyler. Such was the sport's success that the bikes he had customised were in great demand, and his career as a bike designer took off. Haro was becoming more and more famous for his talent, both as a rider and a designer, even appearing as a stunt rider in Steven Spielberg's *E. T. the Extra-Terrestrial*. However, in 1984, after seven years at the cutting edge of freestyle riding, Haro retired from the sport due to a series of knee injuries. He also said that he wanted to be remembered at his peak as the best in his field, rather than fading away. Haro now focuses his energies on his design and marketing company, Haro Designs, Inc. In 1987 his contribution to the biking world was formally acknowledged, when he was inducted into the American Bicycle Association Hall of Fame.

BITS AND PIECES...

- The first clipless pedal was invented in 1895 by Charles Hanson. Like its modern-day counterpart, Hanson's pedal worked on the 'twist-and-lock' principle and even had a float.

- Legendary Italian cycling brand Campagnolo, founded by Tullio Campagnolo in 1933, is responsible for some of the greatest innovations in modern cycling, having introduced the group set, the derailleur and the quick-release wheel.

- Celebrated by cyclists worldwide as one of the most comfortable and hard-wearing perches money can buy, Brooks saddles are hand-made with quality leather, and as such become more comfortable the more they are ridden. The company's classic designs have changed little in over a hundred years.

Truly, the bicycle is the most influential piece of product design ever.

HUGH PEARMAN

The bicycle is a curious vehicle. Its passenger is its engine.

JOHN HOWARD

FEMME CYCLISME

Let me tell you what I think of bicycling. I think it has done more to emancipate women than anything else in the world. It gives women a feeling of freedom and self-reliance.

SUSAN B. ANTHONY,
AMERICAN CIVIL RIGHTS CAMPAIGNER (1820–1906)

Although, like many sports that have developed into multi-million-pound industries, the professional side of cycling is largely dominated by coverage of male athletes in events like the Tour de France, women's cycling has a history as proud and revolutionary as that of men's. From the early days of the bicycle when women (and men) were offered the opportunity to travel to neighbouring towns and villages and socialise with a wider circle of people, to the widespread female participation in every type of competitive cycling today from downhill mountain biking to track racing, there is certainly no lack of involvement when it comes to women of all ages taking to two wheels.

THE GREAT EMANCIPATOR

The bicycle revolutionised the daily lives of countless numbers of people when it became widely available, by broadening their horizons, but this effect was arguably even more significant for women than men. Cycling gave women a new way to express an identity of independence that had not previously been able to develop on a wide scale.

Figures such as Tessie Reynolds who, in 1893 rode from London to Brighton on a 'man's' (horizontal-barred) bike wearing cropped breeches, and Annie Londonderry who in 1894 attempted a round-the-world trip with her bike, were two women among many who had begun to strive for equality through the bicycle, showing the world that they too could exploit the potential of the machine to its fullest, experiencing what suffragette Susan. B. Anthony called 'free, untrammelled womanhood'.

She who succeeds in gaining the mastery of the bicycle will gain the mastery of life.

FRANCES E. WILLARD, *HOW I LEARNED TO RIDE THE BICYCLE*

I was nearly sick. But that's how you have to ride – as if you never want to breathe again.

EMMA POOLEY ON WINNING SILVER AT THE BEIJING OLYMPICS

STEPPIN' OUT

Back in the days when a lady was expected to comport herself with dignity and grace, female cyclists favoured bicycles with what would later be referred to as a 'step-through' frame. The step-through frame, with its downward sloping (or sometimes absent) crossbar was intended to ease the act of mounting and dismounting which – for those women who preferred to ride in a skirt or a dress – was ideal in that it reduced the awkwardness of getting on and off the bike.

While it succeeds in practicality, though, a bike of this sort falls short in the integrity of its design: the weight-bearing properties of the classic 'diamond' design are compromised, meaning the bike's frame is less efficient in transferring the energy generated while cycling. Furthermore, the angled crossbar is longer than that of a horizontal one, and as such requires more material, making the bicycle a little heavier.

Today, though many bikes are still designed with gender-specific features, step-though frames and the classic diamond-shaped frame are enjoyed by men and women alike – you can simply choose whichever one rings your (bicycle) bell!

*I relax by taking my bicycle apart
and putting it back together again.*

MICHELLE PFEIFFER

*The bicycle is just as good company as most
husbands and, when it gets old and shabby,
a woman can dispose of it and get a new one
without shocking the entire community.*

ANN STRONG, *MINNEAPOLIS TRIBUNE*, 1895

KEEPING UP WITH THE BOYS

Many new cycling fans may be surprised to learn that there is in fact a women's Tour de France, known as Le Tour de France Féminin or simply the Grande Boucle (the big loop). The women's Tour was established in 1984 and, like its male-only counterpart, it attracts the best female cyclists from around the world.

That other giant of cycling events, the Giro d'Italia, also has its female equivalent. The Giro d'Italia Femminile (or Giro Donne), perhaps unsurprisingly, has largely been dominated by the Italians, with rider Fabiana Luperini taking five wins between 1995 and 2008.

No doubt about it. Because of the power workouts and short, intense efforts, trackies have the biggest butts in the business.

NANCY NEELY

FAMOUS RIDER: MARGUERITE WILSON (1918–)

Affectionately known as Britain's first lady of cycling, Marguerite Wilson set numerous national time-trial and distance records during her impressive cycling career.

As a 20-year-old amateur, Marguerite broke three records on the Women's Road Records Association list in 1938, and went on, a year later, to break 11 more, also becoming a professional rider for Hercules Bicycles. This already exceptional succession of achievements peaked in 1939 when she claimed the 'End to End' Land's End to John O'Groats record by completing the 870-mile ride in 2 days, 22 hours and 52 minutes. As part of the same ride she also made a new record for covering 1,000 miles, setting a time of 3 days, 11 hours and 44 minutes. It was reported that as she approached the town of Wick, where her marathon ride was to end, there were no lights to be seen as the town was blacked out in anticipation of an air raid.

Marguerite's cycling career continued until 1941, after which, in 1948, she took on the comparatively less exhausting task of working as a stewardess for the British Overseas Airways Corporation.

In 1947 her cycling prowess earned her a place in the famed *Golden Book of Cycling*, created in 1932 by British magazine *Cycling*, which celebrated 'the outstanding rides, deeds and accomplishments of cyclists, officials and administrators'. A shining example of cycling's ability to inspire valour and determination in adversity, Marguerite is rightly considered by many to be the greatest lady cyclist in history.

I was trying to introduce myself as America's woman champion, but I said the French word champignon, so I introduced myself as a mushroom.

NANCY NEIMAN BARANET

The bicycle will accomplish more for women's sensible dress than all the reform movements that have ever been waged.

FROM *DEMOREST'S FAMILY MAGAZINE,* 1895

BITS AND PIECES...

- Cycling during pregnancy is a great way to reduce stress and promote a good night's sleep, though you should always check with your GP before taking any exercise when you're expecting. You may find that you need to adjust your saddle and handlebars to accommodate your extra weight and keep yourself more upright.

- Supermodel Lily Cole, Madonna, and poster girl for the Barclays Cycle Hire scheme Kelly Brook are a few among many female celebs who have been known to opt for two wheels.

- Although female cyclists have a proud history in Europe, the women of Saudi Arabia are not so fortunate, as cycling for women on public roads in this country is not a 'sanctioned activity'.

KINGS OF THE ROAD

*I will get there first, or they will
find my body on the road.*

<small>JAMES MOORE BEFORE WINNING THE FIRST CITY-TO-CITY BICYCLE
RACE, PARIS-ROUEN IN 1869</small>

Of all the cycling stereotypes, the 'roadie' is perhaps the most quintessential. Although he might appear painfully uncool when dressed from head to toe in impossibly tight clothing, waddling around in Velcro-fastened shoes talking endlessly about the latest carbon fibre component that might shave a second off his training time, underneath it all there is a rider with a passion for bicycles and cycling.

Admittedly, road cycling and road racing – with its obsession with speed and optimum performance – can often appear to be the same thing. People may presume that if you're riding a carbon fibre road bike wearing typical road-riding kit you're some sort of fanatic, but for many it's not about the geekish detail of lightweight alloys and shaving seconds off your personal best time for a 50-mile sportive but simply taking advantage of technology that makes your ride more exciting and enjoyable.

Racing fans no doubt relish the fact that Britain has produced some world-class competitors, who can show the continental Europeans a thing or two when it comes to competitive cycling. High-profile riders like Mark Cavendish are an inspiration to die-hard Tour fans and curious non-cyclists alike.

Whatever your preconceptions of roadies are, you can be sure that their enthusiasm comes from a heartfelt love for cycling in its purest form: the bike, the rider and the open road.

*You often meet your fate on the
road you take to avoid it.*

FRENCH PROVERB

It never gets easier, you just go faster.

GREG LEMOND ON CYCLE RACING

THE ROAD MACHINE

Drop handlebars: perhaps the most distinctive feature of the road bike. Even in the late 1800s bikes designed for racing had drop bars to allow a more aerodynamic riding position, resembling modern-day brakeless track bikes.

Lightweight frame: carbon fibre, titanium and aluminium are some of the lightweight materials used for road bikes today – a far cry from their steel ancestors of yesteryear.

Narrow wheels: a reduced rim width, with smooth tyres which maximise surface area contact and minimise rolling resistance (drag between the tyre's surface and the road's) are favoured for road bikes.

Multiple derailleur gears: unlike the first road-riding competitors who tackled every contour with just a single gear, modern road machines tend to feature a cassette of gears to help the rider vary his pedal speed and power for different stretches of the road.

A road rider who is not practised is merely an athlete on a bike, half-educated, a pedaller...

MAYNARD HERSHON

We're hated on the roads. We just hope people realise we are just flesh and bones on two wheels.

VICTORIA PENDLETON ON ATTITUDES TO CYCLISTS IN THE UK

GETTING SPORTIVE

Cyclosportives are essentially the cycling equivalent of marathons, in which participants race against the clock to complete a pre-planned long-distance route, ranging from anything between 20 km and 250 km. Even though sportives don't directly pit one rider against another, they will typically feature some challenging terrain in order to test the stamina and riding skills of the competitors.

At a professional level, sportives can be gruelling. La Marmotte in France is a one-day sportive that takes riders through 174 km from Bourg d'Oisans to famed Tour de France location L'Alpe de Huez. Equally as famous and as challenging, the Paris–Roubaix – first run in 1896 – has earned the nickname *L'Enfer du Nord*: The Hell of the North. One of the hellish aspects of the race is the cobblestone (or, more precisely, 'sett') sections, which shake both rider and bicycle as they pass over them, often leading to untold mechanical faults and injuries.

On the other hand, many more amateur and down-to-earth sportives exist and they are a great way to indulge your competitive streak and get a taste of road racing – there are many such events that take place throughout the UK. Check out www.cyclosport.org for an extensive list of sportives worldwide.

A TASTE OF LE TOUR

The event that arguably causes most excitement for wannabe sportive pros is L'Etape de Tour (which translates as 'stage of the Tour'). What makes it doubly exciting is that the sportive takes place during the Tour itself, usually in July when the riders are taking a rest day. The course depends on the route taken by stage 10 of the Tour that year, but it regularly takes in legendary locations like Mont Ventoux and the Col du Tourmalet. The race is a dream come true for any rider who longs to put themself in the shoes and in the saddle of some of the sport's legends.

www.letapedutour.com

CYCLING'S OWN SUPERMAN

Whatever your opinion of The Boss, charismatic Texan Lance Armstrong is undeniably one of the most remarkable sportsmen of the twentieth century – perhaps even one of the most remarkable ever.

Dr Edward Coyle of the University of Texas once commented that 'Lance is one in a million... The amount of fatigue-causing lactic acid produced by his cycling muscles is only one-fourth that of his competitors.' In medical terms, then, Lance can be considered a kind of Superman. Like the comic-book hero, though, Armstrong has his enemies: accusations of doping from fellow cyclists and journalists tarnished his reputation, even though to date no allegations have been qualified with hard evidence.

But what really sets Armstrong apart and makes his story the stuff of legend is the triumph of his will – his determination to battle with and finally overcome cancer, his ability to rise above his fellow athletes and win cycling's most challenging and prestigious competition a record seven times, and his strength to show dignity in the face of his critics are all reasons why Lance can be considered a true champion.

Men invented war so they could be among themselves. In peacetime, they have bike racing.

GABRIELLE ROLIN

The bicycle riders drank much wine, and were burned and browned by the sun. They did not take the race seriously except among themselves.

ERNEST HEMINGWAY, *THE SUN ALSO RISES*

BEST OF BRITISH (RETIRED ROADIES)

Chris Boardman: UCI Hour Record (1993, 1996); Olympic Gold, 4 km pursuit (1996); Tour de France, 2 stage wins (1994, 1997)

Ray 'The Boot' Booty: National 100-mile Time Trial in under 4 hours (1956); National time trial winner (1955–1959).

Beryl Burton: Women's World Road Race Championship Winner (1960, 1967); Road Time Trials Council's Best All-rounder (1959–1983); Set 50 new national records for 10, 15, 25, 30, 50 and 100-mile distance time trials.

Brian Robinson: first Briton to complete the Tour de France (1955); first Briton to win a Tour de France stage (1958).

TOUR OF BRITAIN

Although perhaps not as *grand* as its famous French counterpart, the Tour of Britain – formerly known as the Milk Race – follows a similar structure, being a race conducted over various stages that take riders to different parts of the country.

The original impetus of the Tour came from a group of cyclists keen to set up a British version of the Tour de France who, in 1942, formed the British League of Racing Cyclists to rally for the then unpopular cause of organised mass road races.

The moniker 'Milk Race' was first applied to the race when the Milk Marketing Board (MMB) decided to sponsor the nascent Tour of Britain in 1958, after they had the brainwave of convincing riders of the increasingly popular event to wear jerseys with their catchphrase 'Drink more milk' on them. Their sponsorship lasted until 1993.

Today the Tour attracts many up-and-coming professional riders and has been a watershed competition for riders like Mark Cavendish, Andy Schleck and Roger Hammond.

Famous Rider: Tommy Simpson (1937–1967)

Tommy Simpson was one of the biggest cycling stars England has ever seen, being the only Briton ever to win the professional world road race championships, Milan–San Remo, the Tour of Flanders and the Giro di Lombardia, as well as being the first British cyclist to wear the yellow jersey in the Tour de France. At the peak of his career, he had won over 40 professional palmarès (podium spots and other such race listings) – all the more incredible because in the 1960s, English speaking champions were a rarity. He was a teammate and mentor to the future Tour de France winner Eddy Merckx; inspirational for his energy, wit and charm, Simpson had a large following of young cycling enthusiasts. In 1965, he achieved another first – becoming the first cyclist to win the BBC Sports Personality of the Year Award.

However, little more is publicly known about Tommy Simpson's life: regrettably, the events surrounding his untimely death during the 1967 Tour de France have since overshadowed his life and his achievements on the bike. At the age of 16, Tommy wrote a letter to a former cycling great, Charles Pélissier, saying, 'I have been told that if I race often, I will burn myself out, and will be no good when I get older, do you think this is true. Yours in sport, Thomas Simpson.' Tragically, his own prediction came true, as Simpson literally rode himself to death, falling off his bike on Mont Ventoux during the 13th stage of the Tour due to a combination of dehydration, exhaustion and amphetamines (a discovery which sparked the introduction of drug testing in cycling). Simpson's often-attributed last words, 'put me back on my bike', were never actually spoken by him, but, as many people have commented, they echoed his beliefs and relentless energy perfectly. The spot of his death on the mountain – which still occasionally features in Tour de France routes – is marked by a memorial, and is regularly visited by cycling fans wanting to pay their respects. One man apparently cycled up the mountain in suit and tie, declaring, 'I'm dressed as a gentleman because I'm here to meet a gentleman.'

One of the positive outcomes of Simpson's death is an increased awareness of health and safety in road racing. Previously, racers were only allowed four litres of water per day, and drug-taking was common practice. British road champion David Millar said, 'Every time I pass his memorial I am in the habit of doffing what in my younger years was a cloth cap, but has since become a helmet, to his memory.'

SELECTED CAREER HIGHLIGHTS

1956: silver medal in the national individual pursuit; bronze medal in Melbourne Olympic games team pursuit.

1957: gold medal in the British League of Racing Cyclists national hill climb championship.

1962: yellow jersey in the Tour de France stage 12.

1964: fourteenth overall in the Tour de France.

1965: winner of the world road race championship (San Sebastian); winner of Tour of Lombardy; seventh in Paris-Roubaix.

1967: winner in Paris–Nice; winner in the Tour of Sardinia; two stage wins in the Tour of Spain. Fourth, stage 9, Tour de France.

HOW'S ABOUT THIS THEN, BOYS AND GIRLS?

Before his days as a tracksuit-wearing, cigar-smoking, warbling TV legend, Jimmy Savile was a keen racing cyclist. In fact, he was all but professional, taking part in the 1951 Tour of Britain. Presumably this was before his love of outrageous jewellery developed, since this would surely have put him at a disadvantage on his bike – jingle jangle!

A mountain bike is like your buddy.
A road bike is your lover.

SEAN COFFEY

THE ART OF CYCLING

Think of bicycles as rideable art that can just about save the world.

GRANT PETERSEN

The bicycle has, throughout its long and illustrious history, made impressions in some major areas of society, from politics and industry to leisure and sport; however, the bicycle or the act of cycling as the focus for cultural expression or inspiration seems a little far-fetched – after all, a bike is a practical (though relatively stylish) vehicle designed simply to get us from A to B. Doubters should realise, though, that nothing is beyond art or the creative imagination, which can transform the humble valve cap into an excuse for a novelty style accessory or the spoke of a wheel into a 'musical' instrument. Bicycles have inspired countless artistic outpourings, proving that they are truly more than the sum of their parts to artists, too.

Bicycles are almost as good as guitars for meeting girls.

Bob Weir, Grateful Dead guitarist and vocalist

BICYCLE POSTER ART

Like all new products, the bicycle – at the time when it was becoming widely available to the public consumer – needed advertisement. In the latter part of the nineteenth century, when the bicycle craze was taking hold across America and Europe, companies turned to poster artists to help create inspirational images of the bicycle as liberator and mechanical wonder. American companies commissioned high-profile artists such as Edward Penfield (a historic figure in the era of the American poster) and Will H. Bradley (the most highly-paid American artist of the early twentieth century) for their ads, some of which were exquisitely painted. Such posters accounted for up to ten per cent of America's advertising during this period.

ART BIKES

When is a bike not a bike? When it's art, of course! The term 'art bike' may be somewhat vague, but it's commonly used to describe a bike that has had its appearance modified in an artistic way – a papier mâché dragon's head may have been mounted on its bars, along with a tail made from a pair of old tights, or perhaps the bike has been chopped up and re-welded to make an entirely new and unrecognisable vehicle. The possibilities are seemingly endless.

In typically flamboyant (if not slightly baffling) style, Japanese bike owners have, over the years, developed their own indigenous style of art bike, known as *Dekochari* – *deko* being an abbreviation of 'decoration' and *chari* slang for 'bike'. Inspired by a series of movies, *Truck Yaro*, which featured trucks accessorised with rows of lights and glittering chrome (think a pimped-out version of the *A-Team* van) children would try to emulate the impressive looks of the vehicles they saw on screen by bulking up their bikes with plywood boxes and adding lights to them. This has, of course, evolved into a full-blown movement, with all manner of bulked-out, flashing conversions being created by *dekochari* clubs across Japan.

NAME THAT TUNE...

Some bicycle-themed musical highlights of the past 50 years include:

- 'Bicycle Race' by Queen
- 'Bike' by Pink Floyd
- 'Tour de France' by Kraftwerk
- 'The Bicycle Song' by the Red Hot Chili Peppers
- 'Cycling is Fun' by Shonen Knife
- 'The Bike Song' by Mark Ronson & The Business Intl.

ZAPPA PLAYS BICYCLE

Before becoming a guitar legend and all-round musical hero, the famously eccentric Frank Zappa turned his hand to playing the bicycle in a spot on *The Steve Allen Show* in 1963. Looking clean-cut in a suit, shirt and tie the audacious young musician took to the stage and demonstrated to the show's host how to 'play' the bicycle, though most of the sounds were simply made to appear as if they were emanating from the various parts of the bike when touched, blown or struck. At a time when wholesome American TV was still very much a staple, this truly bizarre and avant-garde exhibition was almost too weird to be true!

WHERE BICYCLES GROW ON TREES

In August 2008, holidaymakers in Jakarta may have been intrigued and somewhat baffled to encounter what appeared to be a forest of bicycle-bearing trees. Rather than being some strange new species or art installation however, the eye-catching display was actually part of the Indonesian tradition known as *Panjat Pinang.* Villagers celebrate their country's Independence Day by chopping down nut trees, planting them in the middle of the village and attaching 'prizes' to the tops, before greasing the trunks and inviting groups of people to try and work together to pluck them off, which – in this instance – included fully-assembled bicycles.

A truly bizarre and inspirational scene which no doubt excited onlookers as much as those who were struggling to reach their two-wheeled prize!

BITS AND PIECES...

- In 1961 the IBM 704 made history by being the first computer to 'sing': the song was 'Daisy Bell' by English composer Harry Dacre, which features the famous line about 'a bicycle built for two'.

- Ridley Scott's first film was entitled *Boy and Bicycle*, a black and white short.

- In the movie *Pee-wee's Big Adventure*, in which Pee-wee's trademark red and white cruiser goes missing, no less than 12 vintage bikes were sourced to cover shooting for the entire movie.

- The iconic scene in the blockbuster movie *ET the Extra Terrestrial*, in which leading character Elliott takes flight on his bike while carrying ET in its basket, was voted 'the most magical moment in cinema' by *Empire* magazine in 2004.

The bicycle, the bicycle surely, should always be the vehicle of novelists and poets.

CHRISTOPHER MORLEY

The Tour de France for Beginners

I'll be a fan of the Tour de France for as long as I live. And there are no secrets – this is a hard sporting event and hard work wins it. So vive le Tour forever.

LANCE ARMSTRONG

Whether you're a life-long fan or seeing the action for the first time, it is difficult not to become enthralled by the power, determination and grace of the athletes that do battle in gruelling mountainside ascents, body-breaking time trials and lightning-quick descents in some of the most majestic surroundings in Europe. Sleepy hillside villages, country towns and capital cities are set alight as riders make their way through raving, ecstatic crowds. The hype and atmosphere of the event is so intense as to be bewildering for those who haven't caught the fever, yet there can be no doubt that the riders in the Tour deserve the adulation they receive, having to race for three weeks for a distance of over 3,600 km, with the winner averaging a speed of around 40 kmh. As well as having a proud and illustrious heritage that stretches back over 100 years, the Tour de France continues to make world-renowned heroes of men and their two-wheeled, pedal-powered machines and is rightly celebrated as 'the greatest show on the road'.

Whether it is a road bike or mountain bike or tandem bike. I enjoy riding a bike.

LANCE ARMSTRONG

I don't drink alcohol and I have no time for a girlfriend. My ambition is to participate in the Tour de France.

MATIWOS ZERAY

THE FIRST TOUR DE FRANCE IN NUMBERS

6 – the number of stages in the race – in contrast to the modern Tour, some of these stages were so long that most of them started before dawn – and one even started at 9 p.m. the night before!

19 – the duration, in days, of the race (including up to three rest days between some stages)

471 – the distance, in kilometres, of the longest stage

1903 – the year the Tour was held

12,000 – the value, in francs, of the first prize

THE LITTLE CHIMNEY SWEEP

The winner of the first Tour de France was one Maurice-Francois Garin, born in the mountain village of Arvier, Italy in 1871. Being of a suitably small stature, he worked as a chimney sweep during his early teens and, after moving to Lens in France in 1902, he bought his first bicycle for 405 francs. Garin's first professional racing victory was in a 24-hour, 701-km race in Paris. His recipe for success, it is reported, included lots of strong red wine and hot chocolate, 45 cutlets, two kilos of rice and some oysters, among various other foods. By the time the first Tour de France was announced in new French paper *L'Auto* in 1903 Garin had won several important races, and he went on to eventual victory in this monumental new event. *Le petit ramoneur* became the first in a long line of unforgettable champions, finishing almost 65 hours ahead of the last competitor.

TOUR SPEAK

Peloton: the main pack of riders, from the French term for 'little ball'.

Breakaway: when riders break away from the stability of the peleton, usually for a tactical advantage.

Les domestiques: the French term to describe team riders. Domestiques are those riders who 'take one for the team' and try to keep their team's star rider(s) in a good position during a stage.

Tête de course: this often appears on screen during TV coverage of the Tour to indicate the current course leader.

Lanterne rouge: the rider bringing up the rear is known as the 'red lantern'.

A win is a win. Only you can win normally or you can win with panache.

EDDY MERCKX

It's the only race in the world where you have to get a haircut halfway through.

CHRIS BOARDMAN ON THE DURATION OF THE TOUR DE FRANCE

TOUR DE FRANCE JERSEYS

Yellow Jersey – most regularly referred to as the *maillot jaune*, this jersey is awarded to the race leader at the end of each stage and finally rests with the rider who completes the tour in the quickest time overall.

Polka-dot Jersey – the red-and-white-spotted jersey denotes the King of the Mountains – the best climber on the tour – given to the rider who collects the most points by consistently reaching designated checkpoints on climbing stages ahead of his fellow riders.

White Jersey – this jersey is awarded to the best young rider of the tour (one under 26 years of age) who has the highest ranking in the general (overall time) classification.

Green Jersey – the green jersey is given to the rider who consistently finishes high in the rankings throughout the tour and is again determined by points. Although this requires good all-round ability, it is usually sprinters who win this honour, as they are the ones jostling to finish at the front of the main body of riders (the peloton) in the less mountainous stages of the tour.

UP IN THE CLOUDS

Perhaps the most remarkable stages of the Tour are its mountain sections, where that most hardy breed of cyclist – the climber – is given a chance to rise above his fellow competitors and claim the coveted polka-dot jersey. Rarely a year goes by without the Tour passing through some of France's most stunning landscapes in the Pyrenees and the Alps, and some of the locations have taken on legendary status.

Cutting through the mossy green Hautes-Pyrénées, the Col du Tourmalet is 19 km long with an average gradient of 7.4 per cent and starts at the commune of Luz-Saint-Sauveur. The Tourmalet first featured in the Tour in 1910, crossed for the first time by French rider Octave Lapize who went on to win the competition in that year. A silver-coloured statue of Lapize struggling to make the climb can be found at the top of the route, along with a memorial to Jacques Goddet, a long-running director of the Tour. As well as being one of the most familiar features of the Tour de France, the Tourmalet region is known for being populated by the handsome white-winged snowfinch and for its rustic ewes'-milk cheese.

The winding climb through Alpe d'Huez, located in the Central French Alps, is 13.8 km long and is considered by many to be crucial in deciding the winner of the Tour. It has been nicknamed 'the Dutch mountain', since competitors from the Netherlands have, historically, shown a surprising competence in tackling the ascent. It is renowned for attracting burgeoning masses of feverish spectators, who line the sides of its narrow roads and intensify the already electric atmosphere of the climb. When it's not being swarmed upon by avid Tour de France fans, the Alpe d'Huez functions as one of Europe's premier ski resorts and in 1968 was the venue for the bobsleigh event in the Winter Olympics.

Of all the mountain stages in the Tour, Mont Ventoux is arguably the most notorious. Its barren, almost lunar limestone landscape gives this once-forested mountain an otherworldly aura and, true to its dramatic image, it has been the site of some truly memorable events. The most famous of the routes up the mountain, south from Bedoin, is 21.8 km in length and has pushed many riders to the brink of their physical and mental capabilities. Every Tour de France fan knows the tragic tale of charismatic British rider Tom Simpson who collapsed and died on the mountainside during the 1967 Tour. The mountain also came close to breaking Tour legend Eddy Merckx in 1970, who had to be given oxygen to recover from a collapse during his ascent. Aside from these historical resonances, the Ventoux is famed for being climbed by Renaissance thinker Petrarch who, unlike the riders in the Tour de France, was trying to get to the top simply 'to see what so great an elevation had to offer'.

BITS AND PIECES...

- The winner of the 1988 tour, Spain's Pedro Delgado, received a new car, a studio apartment, a piece of art and 500,000 francs in cash as his prize.

- In 1987 Stephen Roche became the first Irish rider to finish the Tour with the yellow jersey.

- The first cyclist to die while taking part in the Tour was Frenchman Adolphe Hélière in 1910. He drowned after being electrocuted by a jellyfish on a rest day in the French Riviera.

The problem with being a Tour de France winner is you always have that feeling of disappointment if you don't win again.

GREG LEMOND

Learn to swear in different languages. Other riders will appreciate your efforts to communicate. They'll also know who you're talking to.

ROBERT MILLAR ON FITTING INTO A PROFESSIONAL PELOTON

Jack and Jill have just climbed the Alpe d'Huez, one of the steepest peaks in the Alps on their tandem.

'Phew, that was a tough climb' said Jill, leaning over, breathing hard. 'That climb was so hard, and we were going so slow, I thought we were never going to make it.'

'Yeah, good thing I kept the brakes on,' said Jack, 'or we'd have slid all the way back down!'

The Joys of Touring

Nothing compares to the simple pleasure of a bike ride.

JOHN F. KENNEDY

ON THE ALE TRAIL

Cycling through the quiet country lanes of rural France or taking in the spectacular lakeside views of Italy is a fantastic way to enjoy your bike abroad, but before loading up your panniers and taking the first ferry across the channel it might be well worth considering what good old Blighty has to offer in the way of touring treasures.

For those who are fans of the traditional English pub, taking your wheels on a whistle-stop tour can be the ideal way to spend a lazy Sunday (or even a good old-fashioned British holiday taking in the odd B&B).

Chances are your local CAMRA group can point you in the right direction – their regional websites often contain information on bike routes that take in pubs and breweries serving 'real' beer and traditional grub. Check out their website www.camra.org.uk for links to a webpage that covers the real ale pubs near you.

*... amid the delightful surroundings of the great
outdoors, and inspired by the bird-songs, the
colour and fragrance of an English posygarden,
in the company of devoted and pleasant
comrades, I had made myself master of the
most remarkable, ingenious, and inspiring motor
ever yet devised upon this planet.*

FRANCES E. WILLARD, *HOW I LEARNED TO RIDE THE BICYCLE*

It is by riding a bicycle that you learn the contours of a country best, since you have to sweat up the hills and coast down them.

ERNEST HEMINGWAY

I love everything about the machine – the sensation of the tyres on the road, the mobility – and I love the fact that you have this intimate relationship with the elements, and the landscape.

BEATRIX CAMPBELL

CYCLE MUSEUMS AT HOME AND ABROAD

The National Cycle Collection, Powys, Mid Wales: inside the museum's charming Art deco building on Temple Street in Llandrindod Wells, visitors will find collections of bicycles ranging from 1819 to the present day presented in period settings. Eileen Sheridan and Fausto Coppi are two cycling legends who have been celebrated in the NCC's exhibitions.

The Velorama National Bicycle Museum, Nijmegen, Netherlands: this museum is a private collection of veteran and modern bicycles and cycle accessories belonging to its founder, Mr Gertjan Moed. Among the many delights in the collection are bikes with bamboo frames, chain-pull 'spoon' brakes and spring-mounted metallic tyres.

Coventry Transport Museum, Coventry, West Midlands: boasting the largest collection of British road transport vehicles in the world, the museum features many rare and valuable bicycles, including a hobby horse which dates back to 1818 and an example of the infamous Rover Safety Cycle from 1888.

The Bicycle Museum of America, New Bremen, Ohio: in addition to the more familiar high-wheelers and other early bicycles, the BMA has some absolute gems of design, such as the 1936 Schwinn Autocycle which sports a motorcycle-like tank and speedometer, and a 1960 Bowden Spacelander, with a (then) futuristic-looking fibreglass frame shell and miniature propeller on its handlebars – a marvellous celebration of the American flair for bicycle design and engineering.

Travelling on a bicycle allowed me to cover the ground while giving me time to stop and stare, to soak up the views and to meet people who had a tale to tell.

CLARE BALDING, FOREWORD TO *BRITAIN BY BIKE* BY JANE EASTOE

IS THERE SUCH A THING AS 'DRINK RIDING'?

As with most laws, technicalities can cloud any straightforward, yes-or-no answer. Since they are not classed as mechanically propelled vehicles, bicycles don't fall within the same part of the law that governs 'drink driving'. However, according to Section 30 (1) of the Road Traffic Act 1988, 'It is an offence for a person to ride a cycle on a road or other public place when unfit to ride through drink or drugs – that is to say – is under the influence of a drink or a drug to such an extent as to be incapable of having proper control of the cycle.'

Further to this, Section 12 of the Licensing Act 1872 (not often evoked but still valid) states that it is an offence to be drunk in charge of a 'vehicle of carriage' – which includes a bike – on a highway or in a public place.

Though many riders who enjoy cycling home from the pub may never have considered themselves 'unfit to ride' or 'drunk', not being able to cycle in a straight line is a sure sign you should play it safe, dismount and push your bike home.

Within five minutes we are cycling through calm, flower-sprinkled countryside. Pale yellow butterflies flirt with the bluebells in the grass verges; the only sounds are of sheep grazing, insects buzzing...

KAREN WHEELER ON CYCLING IN THE
FRENCH COUNTRYSIDE, *TOUTE ALLURE*

Things look different from the seat of a bike carrying a sleeping bag with a cold beer tucked inside.

JIM MALUSA

'What is a "Bummel"?' said George. 'How would you translate it?'

'A "Bummel",' I explained, 'I should describe it as a journey, long or short, without an end; the only thing regulating it being the necessity of getting back within a given time to the point from which one started. Sometimes it is through busy streets, and sometimes through the fields and lanes.. But long or short, but here or there, our thoughts are ever on the running of the sand.'

JEROME K. JEROME, THREE MEN ON THE BUMMEL

FLYING COLOURS

Cyclists are open-minded. Cyclists are egalitarian. Cyclists share a fellowship of the wheel that can overcome all political, social, racial and economic barriers.
Except for recumbents.

TED CONSTANTINO

WHAT THE DICKENS?

The first recognised cycling club met in Hackney Downs, East London, at the Downs Hotel on 22 June 1870. As the meeting took place just 13 days after the death of Charles Dickens, it was decided to call it the Pickwick Club, and each member would have a nickname from the Pickwick Papers. In 1870, they would participate in club rides of ten or twenty miles on 'boneshakers', weighing 60 lbs with wooden wheels and iron tyres. In 1884, the Pickwick Bicycle Club made an expedition to France which included some hard-tyred safety bicycles and high-wheeled ordinaries.

*Socialism can only
arrive by bicycle.*

JOSÉ ANTONIO VIERA-GALLO, CHILEAN POLITICIAN

SOCIAL CLUB

The first Willesden Cycling Club was formed in 1884, in the days of the old penny farthing bicycle, and flourished as a non-racing social club, famous for its candle-lit runs to the wilds of Harrow and Stanmore. It ceased to exist in 1914, when its members were called away to do battle in the fields of Flanders during the Great War. In 1926, however, after the General Strike, a group of socialists decided to use their bicycles to spread the message of the Labour Party Political Cause in villages near London via political meetings, and formed the Willesden Socialist Cycling Club. But by the following year, members found they enjoyed the cycling as much as the politics, and racing events began with a 25-mile time trial (won by a J. Revill in one hour, twelve minutes and ten seconds). In 1931, the club's name became simply the Willesden Cycling Club.

Go Clubbing!

Club cyclists range from those heading for the velodrome to train for glory, to a few friends out for a spin on a Sunday morning, with perhaps a country pub rather than an Olympic gold as their goal. The Cyclists' Touring Club's website – not just for tourers – offers information on what to expect from joining a cycling club, as well as some suggestions as to how to get involved.

WWW.CTC.ORG.UK

PROPAGANDA PEDALLERS

The Clarion Cycling Club was formed in February 1894 by six young men at the Labour Church in Constitution Hill, Birmingham, who met to discuss how they might 'combine the pleasures of cycling with the propaganda of Socialism'. By the next spring there were four other Clarion Cycling Clubs around the Midlands and North of England, their members totalling 120. Tom Groom, one of the originating members, said that 'the frequent contrasts a cyclist gets between the beauties of nature and the dirty squalor of towns make him more anxious than ever to abolish the present system.' The health benefits and social side of the cycling clubs contributed to the cause, with 'Fellowship is Life' as part of their identity. There were 70 clubs by 1897.

PAVING THE WAY AHEAD

The Bicycle Touring Club formed in the UK in 1878, later renamed the Cyclists' Touring Club, created maps for cyclists, campaigned for cycle access to parks, and in general promoted the safety and pleasures of leisure cycling. By 1899, it had more than 60,000 members. Today the CTC is the UK's national cyclists' organisation and continues to do invaluable work for the benefit of bike users nationwide.

'STYLE NOT SPEED. ELEGANCE NOT EXERTION'

It's easy to forget that before the advent of skintight Lycra cyclewear was considerably more dapper. Plus fours, tweed jackets and canvas saddle bags on a single-speed Hercules were once standards in the gentle art of journeying by bicycle.

As you may guess from their motto quoted in the title above, this is the tack of the Tweed Cycling Club, whose members share a passion for this classic period of British cycling. In this club, nothing is done without a certain degree of style and grace, right down to the ride invitations which come to their recipients on specially printed postcards, courtesy of the good old-fashioned postman. Good show, what?

WWW.TWEED.CC

The wind is always blowing, shut up and ride.

MOTTO OF AN ATLANTIC BEACH CYCLING CLUB

The bicycle is the common man among vehicles.

JAMES E. STARRS

Taking the High Road

*The best rides are the ones where you bite
off much more than you can chew,
and live through it.*

DOUG BRADBURY

THE ONLY WAY IS UP

It's not only the awful British weather, dodgy road surfaces and rogue sheep that can cause problems while out on your bike – an unexpected gradient can put a dampener on a ride if not tackled appropriately. If you're out for a pleasure ride you'll no doubt prefer to get off and push if a hill gets too much, but for those out to put their body to the test a good technique is what's needed to conquer the col.

Aside from a good level of general fitness, there are certain aspects of your climb that can be concentrated upon to get you to the top before you simply have to take a break. Taking an easy approach to the climb – that is, not attacking the hill fiercely from the outset – will mean that you won't burn energy too quickly; as anyone who climbs hills regularly will tell you, the stretch just before the summit is most often the hardest.

To avoid 'maxing out' and reaching your maximum heart rate/anaerobic tolerance level too soon try to take full, steady breaths rather than panting. Your pedalling should be swift and regular, and it's best to tackle the climb on a smaller gear ring as this will allow you to keep up the tempo. Staying upright is more efficient when climbing, as it reduces excessive side-to-side motion which wastes energy. Being too rigid, though, is not helpful – ideally, your arms should be taut but flexible, allowing the strain of pulling at the handlebars to be lessened.

Finally, there is a degree to which a successful climb depends on 'thinking yourself to the top' – that is, being determined and maintaining a positive mental attitude.

Pain is a big fat creature riding on your back... The steeper the climb, the deeper he digs his jagged, sharp claws into your muscles.

SCOTT MARTIN

THE CATFORD HILL CLIMB

The Annual Catford Hill Climb is perhaps the UK's most renowned and revered hill climb competition. It also holds the honour of being the world's oldest hill climb event, dating back to 20 August 1887 when it was held on Westerham Hill in Westerham, South London. The climb is still held in the spectacular undulating countryside of the North Downs and continues to attract that impressive breed of cyclists for whom the punishing physical and mental efforts of such gut-busting gradients satisfy a rare but inescapable appetite.

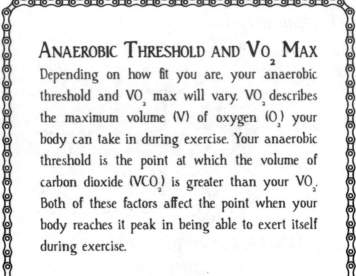

ANAEROBIC THRESHOLD AND VO_2 MAX

Depending on how fit you are, your anaerobic threshold and VO_2 max will vary. VO_2 describes the maximum volume (V) of oxygen (O_2) your body can take in during exercise. Your anaerobic threshold is the point at which the volume of carbon dioxide (VCO_2) is greater than your VO_2. Both of these factors affect the point when your body reaches it peak in being able to exert itself during exercise.

To climb steep hills requires slow pace at first.

WILLIAM SHAKESPEARE, *HENRY VIII*

Wind is just a hill in gaseous form.

BARRY McCARTY

HOLY MOUNTAIN

Atop Madonna Del Ghisallo hill near Lake Como in Italy sits a small and intriguing chapel, in which relics from the world of cycling are placed next to those from the world of religion. The chapel is in fact home to the shrine of Madonna Del Ghisallo, who in 1949 after a blessing from Pope Pius XII was named as the patron saint of cyclists.

Consequently, cyclists from far and wide make a pilgrimage to the chapel, whether it be to view the collection of cycling artefacts – which includes Fabio Casartelli's 1992 Olympic bike, as well as those once ridden by Felice Gimondi and Eddie Merckx – or to pay their respects to the Madonna and maybe pick up a blessing or two for their next big ride.

Nearby the chapel is the Museo del Ciclismo, which contains a huge range of exhibits charting the heritage of Italian cycling.

Chapel of Madonna
del Ghisallo

I had been familiar with that street for years, and had always supposed it was a dead level; but it was not, as the bicycle now informed me, to my surprise... I was toiling up a slight rise, but was not aware of it. It made me tug and pant and perspire; and still, labour as I might, the machine came almost to a standstill every little while. At such times the boy would say: 'That's it! Take a rest – there ain't no hurry. They can't hold the funeral without you.'

MARK TWAIN, *TAMING THE BICYCLE*

FIVE FAMOUS CLIMBS IN THE UK
(IN NO PARTICULAR ORDER)

Great Dun Fell – the second-highest hill in the Pennine range.

Cragg Vale – the B6138 to Cragg Vale in Yorkshire is the longest continuous gradient in England. It rises 968 ft over 5.5 miles.

Porlock Hill – this hill in Somerset makes up part of the A39 and climbs around 1,300 ft in less than 2 miles

Box Hill – by no means a killer for the experienced climber, but one of the most beautiful cycling spots in the South East.

Bealach Na Bà – perhaps Britain's toughest hill: this mountainside pass in Scotland climbs 2,054 ft.

Really steep climbs are not my forte, so I always dread that lowest gear because I figure, god, I'm doomed.

JULI FURTADO

THE URBAN JUNGLE

The sound of a car door opening in front of you is similar to the sound of a gun being cocked.

AMY WEBSTER ON THE PERILS OF URBAN CYCLING

THE CYCLIST'S FRIEND

TRAFFIC LIGHT STRATEGY

- Try to time your arrival just as the light turns green – slow down and aim to keep some momentum going. If you need to stop, change down a gear so you'll have an easier start.

- Weave your way slowly and carefully to the front of any stationary vehicles. Often, in busier more cycle-conscious cities, there are boxes marked out on the road in which cyclists can wait ahead of the traffic. If there isn't one of these areas it's a good idea to make sure you wait in plain view of vehicles behind and in front of you, making your presence known by waiting in the middle of the lane.

- Remember: if you're on a bike you can always save time by getting off, walking around the lights, and getting back on.

What do you call a cyclist who doesn't wear a helmet? An organ donor.

DAVID PERRY

The city needs a car like a fish needs a bicycle.

DEAN KAMEN

LIGHTEN UP

For commuting and shopping by bike in urban areas, the easiest way to carry a heavy load is on the bike, not on your back. Invest in panniers, a handlebar bag or a seat pack. When packing, try to distribute weight evenly; front panniers should carry less weight than rear, because they affect steering and control. If there's a high chance of heavy rain, waterproof pannier covers can be used.

Even though the rapid disappearance of paper means they have less and less to deliver, no other cyclist is as romanticised as the Messenger.

EBEN WEISS, *BIKE SNOB*

BEAT THE BANDITS

It might not seem like the most exciting thing to spend your money on, but ensuring you have an effective lock (or two!) is paramount to keeping your bike safe and secure. In the UK the Association of Chief Police Officers (ACPO) has devised a system of rating the safety of bike locks that have been field-tested using techniques most commonly employed by bicycle thieves; they give the locks they test a Bronze, Silver or Gold rating.

As well as ensuring you have a sturdy lock, you should make a note of your bike's serial and frame number and enter them into a property register such as immobilise.com – you can even upload photos to help police identify your bike should it be stolen.

Remember to use your lock at all times!

For safety is not a gadget but a state of mind.

ELEANOR EVERET

BE SMOG SMART

Air pollution is a fact of urban life, and while motorists are sitting pretty with the air-conditioning on, cyclists are sucking up an exhaust-fume cocktail. If you're an occasional city cyclist, making brief trips here and there, your exposure to pollution will be negligible. However, if you commute on a daily basis at peak traffic times then you might do well to consider taking measures to reduce the amount of fumes entering your lungs.

1. **Check out the air quality in your area:** a marvellous website – www.airquality.co.uk – allows users to access data on air quality in an extensive range of locations throughout the country. Using the site to check when and where air pollution is at harmful levels gives you the option of avoiding high-risk locations. It may add some extra time to your journey or mean that you have to get up a little earlier, but small changes to your route could lead to big benefits for your body.

2. **Wear a mask:** there are plenty of anti-pollution masks designed especially for cyclists. A mask may feel a little strange on your face, but it's a straightforward way of curbing your intake of those nasty fumes.

3. **Don't get stuck in a jam:** naturally, if you're stuck behind a never-ending row of cars spewing exhaust fumes you're more likely to get a faceful, so try to anticipate the queues and avoid them, perhaps by taking an alternative route or by simply dismounting and wheeling your bike through the jam on the pavement.

*You burst off the green like a
surfer on a wave of metal.*

CHIP BROWN, 'A BIKE AND A PRAYER' IN *7 DAYS* MAGAZINE,
ON CYCLING THROUGH TRAFFIC LIGHTS

BITS AND PIECES...

- *Friends* favourite Jennifer Aniston once worked as a bicycle messenger before she became an actress.

- Copenhagen is a fine example of a city which has made cycling work. Some 35 per cent of journeys in Copenhagen are made by bike (the figure for London is 2 per cent).

- Eric Claxton, architect of Stevenage New Town, designed Britain's first network of segregated cycleways in 1946 using his home town as a model. As a result, Stevenage is the only town in Europe with just one set of traffic lights – so that a cyclist's progress should not be hampered.

Brains before beauty: wear your helmet!

ANONYMOUS

I must have been the happiest boy in Liverpool...
the first night I even kept it by my bed.

JOHN LENNON ON GETTING HIS FIRST BICYCLE

I have seen it stated that no expert is quick enough to run over a dog; that a dog is always able to skip out of his way. I think that that may be true; but I think that the reason he couldn't run over the dog was because he was trying to. I did not try to run over any dog. But I ran over every dog that came along. I think it makes a great deal of difference. If you try to run over the dog he knows how to calculate, but if you are trying to miss him he does not know how to calculate, and is liable to jump the wrong way every time. It was always so in my experience. Even when I could not hit a wagon I could hit a dog that came to see me practise.

MARK TWAIN, *TAMING THE BICYCLE*

WORDS WELL SPOKE-N

If I can bicycle, I bicycle.

SIR DAVID ATTENBOROUGH

Give a man a fish and feed him for a day...
Teach a man to cycle and he will realise
fishing is stupid and boring.

DESMOND TUTU

Bicycling is the nearest approximation
I know to the flight of birds.

LOUIS J. HELLE JR, *SPRING IN WASHINGTON*

*There are three ways to pedal a bike:
with the legs, with the lungs,
or with the heart.*

MANDIBLE JONES

*The first Christmas present I remember wanting
so badly it hurt was a bicycle.*

CLARE BALDING, FOREWORD TO *BRITAIN BY BIKE*

The bicycle has a soul. If you succeed to love it, it will give you emotions that you will never forget.

MARIO CIPOLLINI

The cyclist is a man half made of flesh and half of steel that only our century of science and iron could have spawned.

LOUIS BAUDRY DE SAUNIER

Melancholy is incompatible with bicycling.

JAMES E. STARRS

Often he would do a job for me without pay,
because, as he put it, he never saw a man
so in love with his bike as I was.

HENRY MILLER, *MY BIKE AND OTHER FRIENDS*,
ON THE MAN WHO USED TO DO HIS REPAIRS

Be at one with the universe. If you can't do that, at least be at one with your bike.

LENNARD ZINN

Resources

Websites:

www.airquality.co.uk – offers extensive information about the levels of air pollutants in an area near you, searchable by region.

www.bikeradar.com – another wonderful website with a wealth of information for all kinds of riders.

www.britishcycling.org.uk – the website of the UK's national governing body which has information on everything from places to ride to finding a cycling club or event in your area.

www.copenhagenize.com – an inspirational blog based on the Danish city's efforts to become less car-clogged by convincing its citizens to transport themselves by bike.

www.ctc.org.uk – the UK's national cyclists' organisation and an extensive online information centre jam-packed with resources.

www.cycle-route.com – handy for when you fancy a change of scenery but aren't sure of the way. Features a do-it-yourself planner that calculates the distance of your route.

www.cyclosport.org – up-to-date news and details on upcoming sportives in the UK.

www.letapedutour.com – visit this site to learn more about how you can enjoy a taste of the Tour on your own bike!

www.letour.fr – official site of the Tour de France, offering all the latest news and info.

www.road.cc – one of the web's leading websites on all things cycling, with news, reviews and features.

www.sustrans.org.uk – a campaigning organisation that works towards making greener travel choices more likely and more acceptable.

www.tweed.cc – official site of the Tweed Cycling Club.

MAGAZINES:

Cycling Plus – the UK's leading cycling publication.

Cycling Weekly – one of the longest running cycling publications in the UK, still going strong.

Pro Cycling – an inside look at professional cycle racing.

Rouleur – lavishly produced magazine with exquisite photography and passionate reportage.

BOOKS:

BikeSnobNYC *Bike Snob: Systematically and Mercilessly Realigning the World of Cycling* (2010, Chronicle Books)

Eastoe, Jane *Britain by Bike: A Two-Wheeled Odyssey Around Britain* (2010, Batsford)

Enfield, Edward *Dawdling by the Danube: With Journeys in Bavaria and Poland* (2008, Summersdale Publishers)

Enfield, Edward *Downhill All the Way: From La Manche to the Mediterranean by Bike* (2007, Summersdale Publishers)

Enfield, Edward *Freewheeling Through Ireland: Enfield Pedals the West Coast* (2006, Summersdale Publishers)

Enfield, Edward *Greece On My Wheels* (2003, Summersdale Publishers)

Fotheringham, William *Cyclopedia: It's All About the Bike* (2010, Yellow Jersey)

Guise, Richard *From the Mull to the Cape: A Gentle Bike Ride on the Edge of Wilderness* (2008, Summersdale Publishers)

Guise, Richard *Over the Hill and Around the Bend: Misadventures on a Bike in Wales* (2009, Summersdale Publishers)

Guise, Richard *Two Wheels Over Catalonia: Cycling the Back Roads of North-Eastern Spain* (2011, Summersdale Publishers)

Penn, Rob *It's All About the Bike: The Pursuit of Happiness on Two Wheels* (2010, Particular Books)

Warren, Simon *100 Greatest Cycling Climbs: A Road Cyclist's Guide to Britain's Hills* (2010, Frances Lincoln)

Zinn, Lennard *Zinn and the Art of Road Bike Maintenance* (2009, VeloPress)

Two Wheels over Catalonia

Cycling the Back Roads of North-eastern Spain

Pyrenees

Barcelona

Mediterranean Sea

Richard Guise

TWO WHEELS OVER CATALONIA

Cycling the Back Roads of North-eastern Spain

Richard Guise

ISBN: 978 1 84953 144 3   Paperback   £8.99

'This is just the book to whet the appetite of the fairly adventurous but not too strenuous cyclist'

Edward Enfield

Sixteen years after first moving to Catalonia, Richard Guise finally finds time to slow down and explore the back roads by bicycle. With over 400 kilometres of sparkling Mediterranean shoreline and an interior dominated by the Pyrenees, it's a spectacular journey from wind-blown headlands to the glitzy *costas*, and from bustling Barcelona to remote hillsides where only grazing goats and chirruping cicadas disturb the tranquillity.

Dipping into the unique history of this fiercely independent nation-within-a-nation, he uncovers many of its cultural peculiarities, such as why the *sardana* dance is not as easy as it looks and what to do in a *bugaderia*. Stumbling upon nudist beaches, ancient Iberian sites and revolutionary road-sweepers, this slow cyclist revels in authentic Catalonia.

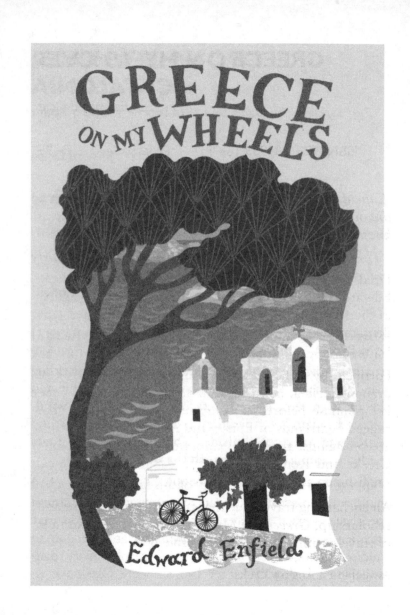

GREECE
ON MY WHEELS

Edward Enfield

GREECE ON MY WHEELS

Edward Enfield

ISBN: 978 1 84953 168 9   Paperback   £8.99

'*Enfield not only impresses – he informs and delights…
the overall effect is charming… it will give you a bit of
knowledge and a warm glow*'   WANDERLUST

Fired by a long enthusiasm for all things Greek,
Edward Enfield mounts his trusty Raleigh to follow
in the footsteps of such notable travellers to Greece as
Benjamin Disraeli, Edward Lear and the Romantic poet
Lord Byron.

Fortified by delicious fish dinners and quantities of
draught retsina, he tackles the formidable roads of the
Peloponnese before plunging, on a later trip, into the
rugged heartlands of Epirus and Acarnania. His travels
are set against the great panorama of Greek history –
Greeks and Romans, Turks and Albanians, Venetians,
Englishmen and Germans all people his pages.

An enchanting travelogue that combines wit, charm and
scholarship, *Greece On My Wheels* is a superb example
of travel writing at its unforgettable best.

Available 1st August 2011

www.summersdale.com